AF226086

THE TSUNAMIC DANCE OF GOD

VELLIYODAN

SHORT STORIES

Translated by
P. Ramgopal

Published By: **Gulf Book Services Ltd,**
20-22 Wenlock Road, London.
NI 7GU
UK
Email: info@gulfbooks.co.uk

ISBN: 978-1-7384322-2-6
Year: November 2023

Author's Note

I look at writing as a spiritual engagement. To me stories are the reflection of devotion to God. My prayers, agonies and wounds get transformed into stories. My life has been a voyage along with writing from the childhood itself. When I was transplanted to the third space at a particular state of growth, my thoughts also were about the human beings of this space. Along with those finding life at the face of catastrophe, those lamenting the loss of space became my characters and stories. Hence, I believe story and life mutually intersperse in my writings. I try to share such stories with the readers in this collection: The Tsunamic Dance of God

These stories are the simple record of people who live with me. They were first published in Malayalam, then, translated into Tamil and later into English.

There are a lot of intimacies I can recollect with the spirit of love:

The great Tamil writer Subrabharathi Maniyan, whose greatness of love could be felt in the reading of the Tamil version;

Prof. P. Ramgopal, who translated it from Tamil into English;

My heartfelt felt thanks to Mr. Madhavan Menon and Gulf Book Services for publishing this book and Mr. Siju Ravi who lead me to the Gulf book Service;

My intimate friend and Delhi university faculty, Dr. P. K. Yasar Arafat, who was always with me, writing the first review in Malayalam and a 'nano' critique on the English version;

My poet friend Mr. Sony Jose Velookkaran, who rendered his valuable assistance in proof reading in English;

The writer Sabeena M. Sali who always has been along with my heart;

Mr. Yoosaf Kulachal who showed the path to Tamil from Malayalam;

R. Muthumani, who translated it into Tamil.

Let me pour out the nectar of love to each of them.

My prayers are these stories be milestones in the flow of time.

With love,
Velliyodan

Preface

The Wounds that can't be Healed by Time

It's an interesting experience to read the creative writings of writers who live abroad. This is because they reflect the different cultures and experiences. In the Malayalam literature, such stories are highly successful. We can even say they occupy a considerable space of the Malayalam literature. The reason being a large number of people from Kerala live in foreign countries including the Gulf. Recently, the Malayalam novel Aadu Jeevatham has sold out one lakh copies. (This book is published in Tamil by the publisher Uyirmei)

Velliyodan is from Kerala. He lives abroad. In this collection, Velliyodan has woven his novels in the backdrops of countries like Sri Lanka, Thailand, Iran and Myanmar. Not only the stories are very interesting to read but they disturb our thinking too. The collection also contains stories sown in Indian soils like Kerala and Mumbai.

The story, The Trees of Sea generalizes in one way or other, the problems of the refugehe es face throughout the world whether they are Indians or others. It talks about people who wander in seas in boats seeking asylum in shore after shore. It symbolically declares that this century is a Century of Refugees! This story won an important prize in the competition held for the Malayalam writers of the world. Another story that focuses on the ending days of a renowned Malayalam writer raises many questions about the meaning of Life! The story Muth'a discusses the pathetic condition of young girls who are impregnated by the Arabs, who leave them soon after conception or as soon as their business is over here! We cannot dismiss in toto that such things do not happen in Tamil Nadu; all we can say is that things are not that bad in Tamil Nadu!

The most important feature about the short stories in this collection is that many of them touch the political turmoil that is prevalent in many countries of the world. These include Iraq, Palestine and Srilanka. The 'massage' story told in the background of a foreign country breaks into pieces the hesitation and embarrassment in carving out such stories. It is a story that talks not only about trifles like massaging but goes beyond to touch the political climate of China. The deceptively massaging lady has a thorough knowledge of China's political atmosphere and is not afraid to criticize her government! The conversation she pursues sends shock waves, like her artificial breasts!

The story of Balachandran (Death Root), son of Prabhakaran, the leader of the LTTE speaks about the political problems of Tamil Eelam! The story was published by Kirantha Lokam, a magazine that enjoys the support of the Kerala Government. It's very heartening to see how deeply the Kerala Government honours the spirit of freedom of her writers! Like this story that speaks about the terrorism sponsored by the Sinhalese, many stories in this collection talk about despotism, through the conversations carried out by the characters!

The violence expressed in these stories has many faces! For example, the sexual violence shown to the young girls, by old men from Arabia is a disturbing example! The depths of this type of sexual torture is touched in the story The Betrayal where a young girl escapes from an Ashram only to fall into another worse trap, set by a young man. Here the Web plays the part of the diabolic villain. Another story openly declares, that it's the Muslims who kill most of the Muslims! The Abandoned talks about the problems of a section of Syrians who were driven away from everywhere and not accepted anywhere! It talks about the visa problems of such Syrians! Cinderella asks, "Are there any wounds that can't be cured by Time?" The story tells that such wounds abound in the hearts of the Malayalam writers!

The diction of the stories derives its strength from the words and myths that are essentially Islamic specific, culture wise! Comments on politics and society are sprinkled here and there!

Studded with poetical words that simply glitter like stars, the stories show how dull prose can touch the zenith of vibrant poetic beauty!

Subrabharathimanian
Tirupur, Tamil Nadu, India
(Recipient of the Katha Award from the President of India)

CONTENTS

A 'Nano' Critique:

Stories of Unbridled Pain and Small Hopes

Velliyodan's The Tsunamic Dance of God waters the bruises of our souls. These stories deal with pain. They talk about small moments of happiness. They illustrate the most un-illustratable.. In his stories, one sees the dark howling of the idulan (translation) bird which heightens the fear of nightmarish dreams. Here, the Sea cries and the Sky waits for solace and peace. In this collection of ten stories, the writer brings to light the pain of helpless people in oppressive regimes, the rude face of racial hierarchy, and the absurdity of political violence. Stories show how the annihilation of minority bodies through systematic purging and mutilations attains a new normalcy in a post-truth era. One also sees how fascism begins to acquire a similarity in face, form and tastes across the world.

The Tsunamic Dance of God engages with the social and political predicament of our time, and thus anger and foulness form the major ingredients of the stories in this volume. The writer's thoughts about China as a socialist myth, Srilanka as a valley of death, racial genocide in Myanmar and the weeping face of Buddha have all been captured beautifully by the absurd protagonists who are alienated from their immediacy. In the story, Abandoned, Velliyodan shows us how the Syrian regime behaves like a cannibalistic family, feeding on its own younger children as it kills them with bombs and chemicals. In a different way, these stories develop into nations that seem akin to withered kafilas (caravan), tired and wretched.

These stories talk about Muslims, and definitely assert the importance of self-criticism. It's the hands of Muslims that killed Muslims more than anybody, for a variety of reasons. The author seems to ask - so, who failed - religion or believers?. His Cinderella faces a similar dilemma, but on a different turf, "love".

She reminds me of a friend who often repeated "love never fails, it's the lovers who always fail", and one does not know if through his own death, he failed or succeeded in love. . Like happiness, like hope, love becomes an un-definable unreality in this collection.

With a fascinating collection of ten stories, cutting across regions and language areas, Velliyodan takes us to the labyrinth of everyday (un)realities- alienation, displacements, dispossession, love, marriage, desire to return. And of course, they also talk of some hope. As a writer, Velliyodan emerges as an incredible social observer with a deep anthropological eye, unravelling the layers in each protagonist. I think that this anthology of short stories heralds a shift in the Middle Eastern pravasi literary world, bringing anthropology and the idea of global "connectedness" into the art of storytelling.

P. K. Yasser Arafath,
Historian and Social Critic,
University of Delhi

Death Root

Squatting and bending, Balachandran took that piece of bread from the ground. He was feeling hungry for a long time. He had trained himself to tolerate the intolerable things.

"Perhaps, it is God who has thrown that piece of bread in front of me," he thought. He did not notice who had thrown it before him. "It's a piece of bread thrown by some unknown person in front of a hungry soul. It's always very easy to write and talk about the pangs of hunger…it has the taste of tears… but when one feels hungry, it affects not only the body but the soul as well," Balachadran mused over.

Closing his eyes Balachandran asked himself, "How old am I? Twelve, at the most! But why do my thoughts then resemble those of the elderly, matured men? Why am I unable to play cricket or foot-ball like other boys? The difficulties I've walked through might have made my thinking sour, perhaps. The slippery rocks I've encountered in my shortcut might have wiped out my finer tastes!"

He did not examine whether any dust or granules of sand or mud-stains were sticking or not on the pieces of bread that he took from the ground. He bit the pieces with his front teeth and pushed them inside his mouth. Then only, he noticed the two elder brothers standing in front of him.

"May be they are the Ambassadors of God! They might have come with the sole purpose of giving me bread. People used to say that one who gives food is God or God's representative!" Balachandran thought. His dad also used to say so! Perhaps such thoughts gave his dad the courage to do those things which he did, he thought.

Dad! Thoughts about his dad passed through his mind like an electric current. He closed his eyes compulsively and dragged himself out from the thoughts about his father. He raised his eyes up and saw the Ambassadors of God!

They laughed. They gestured him to eat all the pieces but they did not say a single word. Suddenly, one of the brothers put one of his hands on Balachandran's shoulder and made him rise from the ground under the tree.

Only then he asked slowly, "Brother, how long is it since you last took food?"

Balachandran tried to find out which day it was! But he could not! Then he tried folding his fingers one by one and started counting the days…yesterday, the day before yesterday, the day before that…beyond that, he could not go! "I could not remember exactly, may be four or five days," stooping his head down towards the ground, Balachandran replied.

"Some water now and then," he told with some irritation, as though he suddenly remembered it!

"Do you know from where did you get this hunger," the second brother asked. It was only then he noticed that a travel bag was hanging from his shoulder. "Govt…" he gulped that word into his mouth with the remaining piece of bread.

"It has come from your dad!" He did not notice who said those words. Just then a small crust of bread passed through his nostrils. That went around for some time, irritated his eyes, filled them up with tears and then came out, due to air-pressure, through his nose. He coughed and felt some irritation in his eyes. The brothers did not talk. One patted his head, in an attempt to bring out the crusts of bread which got stuck. But nothing came out. The other brother took a water bottle from his bag, gave it to Balachandran asking him to take some water. Then looking straight into the young angry eyes, he said: "Yes! It was from your dad, Prabhakaran, Balachandran!" Balachandran did not reply.

He walked forward with them silently for some distance. He stared at the balls of fire rolling here and there on the way. It was the office of the newspaper Uthayam that was going to ashes. His father took guns; that newspaper, pen, instead. The Sinhalese occupied the Northern parts by force. The brothers turned his attention away from the fire. It was always small embers that become big fires, Balachandran thought. It seemed that many groups were trying to form a coalition to give a new shape to a failed revolution. Jaffna! A Tamil world! That used to be a beautiful imagination! But there was a question he always asked himself: "Why did dad drive the Sinhalese away from Jaffna? He could have believed them and the Malays and could have been friendly with them", Balachandran pondered over.

"Where did you study, in London?" one of the brothers asked, interrupting his thoughts.

He did not reply. They also did not ask again. He knew that when he was studying in London, children of his age were studying guns instead of the alphabet in the boy's wing of the

L.T.T.E. He also knew that many mothers who sent their sons to buy something from the petty shops did not get them back. Once he directly asked his dad, "Why did you plant bombs in Central Market and Public Transport to kill people in bunches?'

Without answering him, his dad diverted into some other topic. He was always like that. He never answered any question. There were times when he hated his dad too.

His dad was a forefront revolutionary leader of an ethnic group. He killed others.

Today, every Tamil had to tolerate innumerable, agonizing humiliations.

They walked into a place that was quite lonely. It was not only lonely but it was so deadly silent that even the air passed through that place dumbly.

"Why did the army kill your dad?"

"These people knew everything, I am certain. But why did they come in search of me? Hands of Fate or God's decree?" Balachandran asked himself.

He did not reply. He knew that it would be pretentious to answer to those people who knew everything already.

His dad used to say, "The Tamils do not act; they only react!" But Balachandran often thought the Sri Lankan Govt. might also think and act the same way. Many a time he had asked himself: "Why are there clashes and killings between the minority and the majority sects in the world?

"Who are you?" he asked them for the first time.

The two men laughed. One brother asked, "Whoever we are, we have given you bits of bread."

"N.G.O? If so, even now there are thousands of Tamils suffering in the North.

Please help them!"

"Tamils! Tamils! That one single thought always runs through all of you! Nothing else," the second brother shouted angrily.

"Yes! Only Tamil blood flows in my veins," Balachandran replied in a raised tone and with a sense of pride too. His face betrayed a little sense of guilt for having said so!

The emotional make up that he was a Tamilian had made him say those words. He knew that people without self-respect had only to be floating like shreds of silk-cotton, in the air. Often, he thought that it all lay in some kind of gravitational force that was called 'one's self-respect'.

"This consciousness about one's class and the zeal for one's identity are the root cause of all 'evils' in the world," commented one fellow calmly.

"No! Such thoughts fill us with a sense of pride," Balachandran retorted. "I'm the son of Prabhakaran, who had spent his entire life in fighting for the liberty and honour of our people," he continued.

"No! it was your dad who killed people in thousands throughout our country. You must feel ashamed for being the son of such a man. We are trying to bring you to a rendezvous at last... but..."

Balachandran did not allow him to complete. He blasted:

"Who are you?"

"Commandoes of the Sri Lankan Army," they flashed out their identity through their faces glowing with a sense of bravery. Gratitude, friendship, respect – all vanished from Balachandran's face that instant. Instead, a sarcastic smile spread over it. He did not utter a single word… they did not speak either.

The man carrying the shoulder bag said, "Remove your shirt!"

"Why?"

"You'll understand everything in a short while!"

Balachandran removed his dirt-stained shirt exposing a smooth chest and a concave stomach! Drops of sweat, filled with dirt, went down below his neck. His trousers were loose. One fellow knelt down to take note of the correct height to shoot him. He put his hands on his shoulders and looked into his eyes. He could see a thin thread of mercy in that brother's eyes.

"Are you Balachandran, Prabhakaran's son?"

"Yes! I am!"

"Are you afraid of death?"

He could not answer. His lips quivered …. He shook his shoulders and asked him to answer.

"I want to live!"

"Why? To reach the target of your failed father?"

"No! I want to live peacefully with my mother! I want to become a scientist!"

Tears gathered up in his eyes and started trickling down!" "We've been sent to kill you!"

Balachandran moved very close to his killer and snuggled to his bosom. But that brother pushed him away, stood up and moved further away from him.

The other brother took a gun from his bag, pointed it straight to Balachandran, closed his eyes and meditated.

Next day.

The eagles that circulated in the Jaffna sky feasted upon the drops of blood and bits of flesh off the bullet wounds.

Muth'a

That little girl was like my little darling! I could not turn my attention from her mischievous, playful activities. She drew lines on the walls with the coin in her hands. On seeing her spoiling the walls of the lawyer's office, her mother, I thought so, gave two light strokes on the legs of the child. They were not painful; still she cried. It was a feigned cry, as my mother used to say. On seeing her crying, I smiled. Not even a single drop of tear! But she cried with her mouth open. Like my darling, she also did not have two front teeth. Perhaps, the old ones might have gone, giving way to the new ones. Weeping, she looked at me. When she knew that I was looking at her, she blushed. Bending her head slightly, she, with feigned anger, twisted her lips and drew doodles with her feet on the ground carelessly.

"I think they are Misiris, I told my friend, Hakeem.

"No. They are Iranians," he told in a firm tone. I thought that he guessed so by their tongue. Her mother was also beautiful like her. Wearing blue jeans and a multi coloured kameez, she hid her hair completely with a hijab. With her there was an old lady who appeared like her mother. Three ladies together, belonging to three generations! I did not know why those three ladies had come to the lawyer's office. Perhaps, some legal problem! May be talaq!

I invited the child with my hand gestures. She did not come. Instead, she stood closer to her mother. I tempted her by showing my pen and mobile. But no use.

I wanted to give her a kiss. A girl child like my darling! I dragged her compulsively from the feet of her mother and embraced her tightly. Hakeem, who was thinking until then about what to discuss with the lawyer even without talking to me, warned: "Don't exceed your limits. She would cling to you more closely… the ladies may chide you. They are Iranians."

I remembered Mahmoud Ahmadi Nejad's braveness then and also Ayatollah Khomeini's tubular thinking. Therefore, I must be careful, I thought. But then, I did not commit any mistake. Perhaps as I was in the lawyer's office, there might be arguments and counter arguments in my mind, I thought. There were no objections either from her mother or her grandma, as expected. Instead, the child's mother gave her permission with a smile.

Blushing and with some disinterest, the child came and stood near me.

"What's your name?" I asked in English, because I knew that most children here learn English before learning their mother tongue, like the Keralites here. I immediately realized that I was wrong. It seemed that she did not know English. She not only did not answer me but was staring at me. I corrected her hair that was a bit wavy. Making her hands move in a rhythm and looking at her face, I sang a song. On hearing the song, she sent a paroxysm of laughter. Of course, she did not know the meaning. Malayalam is foreign to her. Perhaps she might have laughed seeing the mischief in my eyes.

"Maza ismak," I asked with a smile.

"Nadiya Binth Ahmed," her mother answered.

"Why here?" I realized only later, as they did not answer, that it was too much! They were looking at the lines drawn by Nadiya. Perhaps, they were entangled in a legal problem they could not reveal to anyone.

The old lady said, "She is a muth'a child". I could not understand that word. That was a word I hadn't heard so far in the Arabic tongue. I looked deeply into the face of the old woman trying to make her understand that I understood nothing. When she was about to say something, the lawyer's clerk led her into the lawyer's room. Nadiya was snatched from my hand suddenly. I could not understand muth'a. I was a bit confused. I asked Hakeem what the meaning of the word was. From his facial expression, I understood that he too did not know the meaning. After a while, they came out of the lawyer's room.

Hakeem went inside. I seized Nadiya with my hands affectionately as though I had every right and kissed her. She returned the kisses, putting her lovely little hands around my neck. Meanwhile, she twisted both my lips into the shape of a mouse and laughed.

Her mother expressed her surprise and happiness:

"You've become thick friends, eh.?"

"Yes! She looks like my little darling!" "How many children do you have?" "None!"

"Then… darling?"

"My friend's daughter. I like her very much. What's that…muth'a child?" I asked to know the meaning. Just then the old lady came out of the lawyer's room wailing some words in Persian. She and the child walked behind her. I also followed them, urged by some inner feeling. I imagined, for a moment, that we were husband and wife and the child was our daughter. When the button was pressed the lift came up and we stepped in. But my question remained still unanswered. "Muth'a?" I asked the lady as if to remind her. Instead of answering me, she asked me another question:

"To which religion do you belong?"

"Islam," I answered with a single word.

"A Muslim! Still you don't know muth'a?"

"Is muth'a such an important word that every Muslim should never forget in his life? Then no Muslim in Kerala knows the meaning of muth'a," I thought. My father belonged to a family that got converted into Islam generations ago! He used to say that we belonged to a very respectable caste and family. Those caste-thoughts did not vanish even after conversions and the passing of generations!

"Do you know nikah?"

"Yes!" I shot back.

"Then muth'a is another form of nikah!"

She confused me again. Is there another such form for nikah?

I tried in vain to understand the meaning by forming different combinations of letters in my mind.

I was looking at the dead chicken, rotating in the machine in the cafeteria without any feeling. Meanwhile, I noticed that they were moving out in a car.

Without taking much time, I returned to the lawyer's office. Even then Hakeem did not come out of the lawyer's cabin. I told Rafique Icha who was from Kasargode in Kerala that I would give him 50 dirhams to get their phone number from the file. When I rang them I was much afraid... I was talking to ladies. If any problem cropped up, I would be finished. Amidst feelings of fear there was some blind boldness. That's why I phoned her. She agreed to meet me in the Abu Shagara Park, next Thursday evening.

After hearing the long magrib azan of the masjid in Konasarasthan village, Hasan Ali drove his sheep to the pen. He took four pots of water from the pond where the sheep drank water ...that would suffice for the night and the next day. The sands of Konarasthan had tasted only the wetness of washed clothes and the smell of sheep. The sands joined the vagabond air and entered into the far-away cities, perhaps, in search of the young lovers who had left the place. His uneducated wife, Fathima, was ironing clothes to give them to their owners to earn the bread for the next day. The tent slightly swayed because of the wind that blew with the sound of a beetle. Rahiya who was telling stories from the avantha immediately ran out dragging her along with her. Only when the wind left the tent unwounded, they returned. Their dream was to have a house that won't dance in the wind.

After putting the sheep, Hasan Ali did ablution in the water about which he could not be sure whether it was clear or dirty. Then he took the sacred stone that was kept on the Qur'an and started walking towards the masjid. As usual, Rahiya did not bring tea to her father. He looked at Fathima, enquiringly.

"She has come of age! She's 14, you know!" As soon as his wife uttered those words, Hasan Ali thought for a minute and then went out as though he had decided on something. Rahiya was angry with her mother and wondered why she was telling all that to her father. From that day onwards, it became a routine for her father to look at her penetratingly. It appeared as though he doubted whether the tree that was bred in his garden would bear any fruit at all. The days passed fast.

Rahiya heard her father saying, "He is a foreigner!" He knew him through a mullah who came to the masjid to give a sermon on the ashura day.

"Fifty thousand dirhams!

The kalavathi is 60 days. Muth'a"

Rahiya cursed herself. She was angry with God. She hated Him who had made her born a Shia Muslim.

"This life may evaporate drowning me in muth'a. But a thousand mutha's would not equal a single nikah," she thought. That truth threatened her. She was a soul who had to put a full stop to all her expectations. The amount would vary as the period varied from one hour to sixty years. She shredded the threads of love that would weave only a nikah and never a muth'a!

She cried and pleaded with her mother. Her face betrayed her inability to meddle with the strong wires of religion.

"Woman is a huq of man. She is the property of the one who gives money… only a biological tool! Are not feelings of love and affection, the huq of women?" she asked herself. There were no answers to the questions in her heart. The old man was more than 65.

"Don't see the age! I am still potent!" When she heard his words, she felt nauseating.

After sixty Sun-sets, when he returned to his native place, she had missed her periods already.

As a result of muth'a, a sperm had transformed into an embryo."

"Is this not practised in Kerala?" she asked me as I was listening to her, stupefied.

"Not only in Kerala. Nowhere in the world!" I was categorical.

"After Prophet Muhammad's victory of Mecca, he banned this till his last day!" I told her what I'd understood. "Your Government does not know that human rights include the rights of women too!" As I was saying those words Nadiya came running to me and threw her face into my lap: muth'a, nikah, Iran… nothing was visible in that face.

There was only the face of my little darling radiating with pristine beauty!

Notes

1. ashura: the martyr day of Imam Hussain, the 10th day of Muharraam.
2. Avantha, the: an Iranian epic.
3. dirham: UAE currency.
4. haq: property.
5. hijab: a veil traditionally worn by some Muslim women in the presence of adult males outside their immediate family, which usually covers the head and chest.
6. kalavathi: duration/ period.
7. magrib azan: evening prayer.
8. maza ismak: 'What's your name?'
9. Misiri: Egyptian.
10. nikah: Muslim marriage.
11. talaq: divorce.

The Pink Shirt Woman from Guangxi

"It's a biological need, an unavoidable one!"

When my friend said so, I could not think otherwise. Even if it was not so, my decisions would be mostly like that on many occasions. They change always according to the advice and views of others. Being unable to take decisions independently is a shame!

"Okay! But let's have it on some other day!" I could not help saying so.

"If we want to go, we should go today itself. There'll be quite a lot of time to spend. He is an expert in spending the time during holidays.

I'd just arrived from my native place. As I hadn't got my salary yet, I did not have much money. That was one of the reasons for postponing that thing.

"I'll pay. It's enough if you return the money after you get your salary!" He said as though he had understood me.

To become indebted to somebody was a thing, I never liked. I never thought that there was a long distance between me and Death. I always thought that the air surrounding me was filled with the smell of Death. My nose was quite familiar to that smell.

Picking up the edge of my silence, he began to speak.

"At any cost we are going by 5p.m. today evening! He finalised suddenly a decision that was dangling on the verge of indecision. I did not say "yes" or "no". I looked down from the vacant seat at the balcony.

I was looking down from the last floor of that fourteen- storey building. The big vehicles looked like dots. I thought that the span of my vision was only that much!

The fact that not only mine but everybody's vision was like that only, made me ruminate: "Boundary lines were drawn for man's thinking and views, even as the boundaries between nations. Who drew those lines? God? Or the self-proclaimed representatives of God?" I asked myself. Yesterday two priests came to my office. I dragged them wantonly to Theology and Theosadism.

One of them said, "From within me God directed me to go over here! That's why I am here!" As soon as he told those words, I asked him, "Are you a Tirthankara?" To this he did not say, 'yes'; nor did he say, 'no'. Saying that it was already late, he left.

He had hidden all his guile and deceit in his white garb! "When somebody says, Everything is His will!' the listener has to hide his tongue behind his lips," I thought.

He came earlier. He succeeded in dragging me out of my room before 5 p.m.

He told to the Pakistani taxi driver only the words, "Bridge Road'." He took us right there. Vehicles were moving fast in that broad road in all directions. As the place was new to us, we were walking, looking at the buildings.

He said, "They said it's a mezzanine flat in the blue building!" There was no need for us to walk for a long time. We saw the name board that was hanging outside and went in.

The walls were filled with the pictures of herbal plants. The remaining parts of the wall were painted green.

"Hai!" we looked at the direction from which the sound came.

A battalion of ten beauties!

An unnatural smile was pasted on everybody's face. Smiles without light, lit their faces up for a while and vanished.

I could hear the sound of a sword – fight inside my heart. I observed his face closely.

No feeling of guilt disturbed him. Of course, he considered those things a biological need!

In the meantime, he had paid the money for us in the counter.

150 dirhams per person.

I felt as though, from the bottom of my stomach, an electric wave rose up, burnt my intestines, both smaller and larger, then went up to cleave my lungs, burst them out and then went near the heart.

The image of the half-constructed foundation of my house in my village that had to be stopped due to paucity of funds and which was burning hot in summer and freezing cold in winter, rose before me! With this money I could construct two more rows! Two thousand Indian rupees!

He had already gone into a room with a lady from Calcutta.

I, who knew not what to do, could not see anybody standing in front of me.

The lady in the counter said in a loud voice: "Sir! You can choose anybody!"

Their pink T-shirts bore the numbers:

1…2…3

I thought that those were the numbers to note down their labour.

I did not say anything

A Chinese lady came and stood in front of me and asked: "You want massage?"

I nodded my head in a way that did not mean either 'yes' or 'no'.

She took my hands and dragged me into a room.

Light Chinese music was flowing from the ceiling, in soft waves. In the centre of the room there was a mattress on a bench, covered with a clean bed spread. At one end of the bench there was a big hole that can house a human face.

'Please use our underwear!' the notice in the wall said. My heart trembled: "My God! Should I use this woman's underwear?" It did not take much time to understand that it was not so. She opened a packet and gave me a new underwear.

Feeling a bit embarrassed again, I stood before her. I saw a feeling of helplessness and inferiority complex in her face. With a coquettish smile she began talking to me.

"What's your name?"

A flash appeared on her face! "What are you going to do if you know my name?" she retorted. However, she replied: "Jeena."

"Sir! You have come for massage, haven't you? Please remove your shirt," she told me in chaste English. I put my surprise in a questioning look! I already heard that the Communist countries didn't encourage English. From my experience too, I knew that.

The Russians who had lost their lives for ten years under the Communist regime, and the Chinese who had been searching for the meaning of the words 'individual freedom' had suffered under me because of their poor knowledge either of English or Arabic.

Perhaps the authorities might have feared that knowing English would open the windows of the world and then people would know new meanings for words like 'freedom' etc.

She said as though she was answering my suspicion, "I worked in a hotel earlier!" She also started compelling me to take my dress off!

"I need no massage to my body…only to my mind!" I told her standing before her, floating an apish smile, different from others who had stood before her with lustful glee.

"Then?" she stopped halfway and then continued, "relaxation-cum-full body massage and for that only your friend has paid!"

"Why don't we spend the hour talking about you and your country?"

Jeena didn't agree. She started opening the buttons of my shirt one by one and then she began to loosen my pant belt. It seemed to me that the bursting steam of manhood had gone somewhere. I did not experience any sexual arousal either suddenly or gradually. Even though the flood gates were opened wide, my feelings were like the calm and unmoving water in a dam.

I did not know why it was so. I could never take shelter under helplessness.

In the beginning she looked at me as though I was a tiger, ready to pounce on her with its mouth wide open even though she was trying to be friendly a little later!

"You have come taking advantage of my need for money!" She did not say in so many words… but I was frozen with the thought that she might have thought so.

I lay on the wide bench in front of her wearing the underwear, she had given me. She dimmed the electric light. The room was filled with the evening light. A mixed fragrance of jasmine and sandalwood filled the room.

She caught hold of my index finger in the right hand and snapped it in a strange manner. The pleasure of that little pain was like the prick of a pin. That feeling went from the index finger to my brain and aroused laughter. She was doing the same to my palm, its back and my armpits.

"Whose music is this?" I asked her enjoying the exquisite pleasure I felt as her fingers moved over my body that was dried off sweat.

"Sister Leu's," she answered moving her hands all over my body like a skilful lady painter, exhibiting all her skills.

"What kind of music is this?"

"The folk music of our place!"

"Which place?"

"Guangxi." Her Chinese pronunciation stole all my intelligence. I asked her to repeat. As she said, 'Guangxi' again, her face shone with pride.

"Is it near Beijing?" Beijing was the only place I knew in China.

"No!" So saying, she asked me to lie upside down and put my face into that big circular hole. Then she started pressing my back with her fists. She sat on my buttocks with her legs dangling down one on each side of my body. As she was pressing my back with her fists gently, she was also moving her fingers around my ears in a feathery way as though she was digging a canal for my blood to flow.

She pressed against my back, her puffy breasts that were like mounds of flesh "Do the Chinese women have such strong big breasts?" I asked myself.

I was like a chicken burger that was pressed between two buns. I was an Indian, squeezed between the bench and a Chinese woman. From the neck, the fingers started moving up and pressed themselves over the head.

"Guangxi is 1220 miles away from Beijing. We share our border with Vietnam. When she was saying those words, her lips were sharing the borders of my ears. I could not put a question to push the conversation on.

"The Government has given us autonomous status and special rights!

"Why so?"

As if in a move to wipe out my doubt, she changed the position of her fists, and sat straight on my buttocks as if she was sitting on a cushion. Then she orderly 'arranged' the bones in my spinal cord.

I miaowed with a strange sensation that was mixed with pain and joy.

I could not discover whether the purring was the result of sexual joy or its pain.

"They annexed us with China in 1995, as they are demanding your Sikkim and Arunachal Pradesh now.

I started respecting her. She was not a mere paper-flower. She knew History, Politics and everything.

"Why do they want to annex Arunachal Pradesh and Sikkim?"

"Sheer arrogance! What else?"

"The average Indian thinks that China respects law and truth!"

"We kept a foolish-silence over what had happened in Afghanistan, Iraq and Kosovo etc. Did we raise our voice for justice? The echoes of the people's revolutions, the Jasmine Revolution in North Africa and Middle Asia were felt in our country too. The Government crushed those in a crueller way than you foreigners can ever imagine," she shivered.

"How come these things are not reported in the world-press," I did not hide my suspicion.

"Media like Google were banned in our country. All news that went out were censored. The reporters who came from your country and from other countries to telecast the Olympics wrote only about our eating of snakes and beetles. Nobody wrote about how people were made cart-pulling bullocks!" The sweat drops from her cheeks fell on me.

She switched off her position from my buttocks to my soles. She threw away my underwear as one would throw a gauze pad used during labour. She gently moved her hands over the throbbing flesh in my buttocks.

Suddenly, she made a jump, took a bottle of oil that was on the table, poured some of it on my buttocks and gently began to massage. The front side of my buttocks that was hitherto dead, began to pulsate like a mattress on which love was made, would vibrate! She put the bottle back on the table and began to stroke my buttocks gently.

"Are you married?" I could ask only that question at that time – the mind and the body travelled together. That's why I asked her so!

"Yes! My husband is a driver in my native place!" "How many children?"

"That's an unnecessary question to shoot at a Chinese. If we have more than one child, we'll have to pay a heavy fine to the Government. There will be other troubles too!"

She answered all my unasked questions!

"In your country there's only a little difference between the haves and the have-nots. Isn't it?"

She was gently gyrating my buttocks, keeping her hands together even. The rhythm was slowly increasing.

"The difference between one zero and another, is a zero, isn't it?" She answered my question with a mathematical equation.

She straightened and squeezed with her thumb and index fingers, the folds of the skin between my buttocks and thighs. The dance began! It slowly spread its 'tentacles' over my thighs.

"Doesn't your country encourage sex tourism?" She was playing with my calf muscles rolling her fingers over them up and down. I experienced an intolerable pain.

"In our country women are dishes for men. They are men's Joy-Toys. They are channels for men who stand, erected with lust!" When she was uttering those words, she had already completed massaging my soles. She asked me to stand up. Lying on my back, I was floating in heaven.

"I want to know more about China!" I told her without getting up.

She did not answer. She was looking at me angrily. Suddenly she threw her T-shirt away. Then she threw her bra too!

"My God!" I shouted, stupefied. She had duplicate boobs.

Notes

1. Tirthankara: a saviour who succeeded in crossing over life's stream of rebirths and has made a path for others to follow.

The Abandoned

It seemed to Tamajeed that there was still more time for the sunrise. It was always like that if one had some important work. Sleep would not come easily during night. Neither would day dawn quickly!

"Okay! I can say the morning prayer," he thought, even though he had no such habit. But he had to achieve his aim at least with the help of God. What would happen and how, he didn't know.

He should complete everything before the American Congress began.

Tamajeed smelt the jeans he took from the hanger. "It's OK, I can wear it today too! The dirt is only three days' old! How to find time to wash and press the clothes amidst all the commotion?" he asked himself.

"If a house could be found, it would be a great relief. But nowadays no flat is available here in this town. It seemed that 'that' dangerous situation then was far better than what is happening today. One or two roomed flats were easily available here, once. But with the new rule in force, making the rent agreement mandatory for getting the visa, all trouble started. If it is not so, I could have brought them here somehow and put them in a rented house at least!" he pondered over.

He could get a house for rent on one-year agreement only. He should show it to the municipality and get it registered. Then only the visa would be issued.

If he wanted to bring in his mother and his sister, his pay should be 10,000 dirhams. When he came to know that fact he was a bit worried.

"How could one, whose salary is only 4000 dirhams, could get the visa?" he asked himself.

At last he fell at the G.M.'s feet and wept, "Sir! They have started the war there. I must bring them here.!"

"Why not bring your wife only?"

"She won't come without my mother and sister, sir!"

On seeing that the G.M. was leaving the room without saying anything, Umar, a Palestine said, "I if you're a Malabari, they would have issued the visa long back. All Arabs are suffering now. Ya Allah," he heaved a sigh. As the G.M. was from Kerala, Umar said so.

Then he went to the project manager, Um Amjad. He thought that as Um Amjad was an Arab, she could understand his miserable plight.

"Madam, I must save my mother and my wife, somehow,"

he pleaded.

The manager's fingers danced on the telephone numbers fast. It went to the Director, then to the G.M. and so on.

When he got the salary certificate stating that his salary was 10,000 dirhams, he felt happy as though he had crossed over a big ocean.

There was not much traffic on the road. He called the telephone number which he had seen on the tower near the post-office, to know whether there was any vacant flat. He was told that there was only one flat. That too was vacated only the previous day. 22nd. floor. Not bad. Only two rooms! Enough! Better than refugee camps, he consoled himself.

He bought a newspaper and went through.

"Ya Allah!" crying aloud, he closed his eyes.

"Chemical war! How many children! The Government says it's the Liberation Movement. The newspapers repeat it.

When Israel did something what did these people say? They said that Israel was murdering the Muslims en masse. Nobody had fought a crueller war against the Muslims so far, in history.

Only Muslims kill Muslims, more than others. If Asad has to leave the Government, he would kill everybody and destroy everything. He would not leave a single Suri untouched. 'If I can't have, nobody should have' that's his principle," he thought.

When he called the real estate people, they asked him to come immediately. "The rent is 36,000 dirhams per year. 2,000 dirhams advance. 3,000 dirhams monthly rent. I'll have a balance of 1000 dirhams. How am I going to manage, paying for electricity, water etc.?" he asked himself.

"Insha Allah!" Tamajeed told himself. He was like that. Sometimes, his faith in Allah knew no bounds; in other times, he was seized with disbelief and depression.

When he came to the real estate office he saw that the rental section was managed by a Malabari. "Would this Malabari give me that flat?" he doubted. He knew that the Malabaris looked down at the Syrians and the Misiris.

"That may be due to our nature! Sheer arrogance! We looked down upon the people who spoke Hindi and the Bengalis! We sang then, now we have to face the music," he mused.

As expected, the Malabari was not interested in allotting the flat to him. He told that somebody had asked for it already. When he begged, he agreed to help him. But he asked for a bribe of 1000 dirhams. He could not refuse.

He went straight to the Municipal Office with the rent agreement.

A long queue. Mostly Syrians. The LED screens displayed the token numbers one after another. There was much time for token No. 178.

He did not go for lunch as he was afraid that he would miss his turn.

When all the work was over, he went to the cafeteria and ate a sandwich just as a routine. Even though he did not feel hungry, he ate! Then Tamajeed's car flew to the Immigration.

It would work until 7p.m. only. Now itself the time was 4. He attempted many calculations in his mind. He must get the visa for three people and send them the day after.

When the war would start, nobody could say.

"The American war ship is waiting in the Mediterranean Sea expecting Obama's order. The Russian War ship is waiting to help Syria.

If there's a chance, Israel is ready to use her force. Iran also wants to show her might. Asad also will not keep quiet.

America or Russia, whoever bombs, only the Syrians die. Bombs or even chemical weapons may be thrown on the

Syrians at any time. America and Russia are far away!" he thought seriously.

He thought that the condition of Sana was pathetic. They were married only six months ago. He could not even enjoy the honeymoon fully. The company asked him to come after two weeks. His leave could not be extended, they said categorically. There was no other way left to him except to join work immediately.

"I must enjoy the honeymoon leisurely, after she comes here!" Thinking so, he closed his eyes involuntarily. As that scene flooded his closed eyes, Tamajeed opened them all of a sudden, with a shock:

The photograph of that two-year old boy in the newspaper! No wounds in his body except the one that had cut his head into two – the brain had come out and the small eyes were dangling below the nose.

From then on, he was afraid to close his eyes.

"How many people! Till today, more than one lakh people have died. The figure may go up with the civil war. That is the biggest and the worst civil war the world has ever witnessed. No schools! No hospitals! Obama has left the decision to the Congress.

The Congress would meet day after tomorrow! If the congress decides, Obama would bomb! Ya Allah! What to do if one could not live in peace in his own soil? No answer to any question!" he felt.

As he was thinking over one thing after another, he was invited to the immigration counter.

The Rental Agreement. The Salary Certificate. The copy of his Passport.

The filled-in application for the Visa.

The photos of the three women and the copies of their Passports.

Smiling, Tamajeed submitted all the papers at the counter. The officer examined all his papers quickly. He was making a tick mark on all of them, one by one.

He then smiled and said, "We've stopped issuing the visa to the Syrians!"

Notes

1.dirham: UAE currency.
2.Insha Allah: if God wills
3.Malabari: a native of Kerala, a state in India.
4.Suri: Syrian
5.Ya Allah: 'O God!'

The Betrayal

That was a kind of escape. Dhaya thought that way only. She did not know what awaited her at the end of that escape. If she would start thinking about what would happen in the future, she could not escape from that place. There was no place to go!

From the day as far as she could remember, it was only the alms of that ashram that stopped the hunger-sobs of her stomach. Now that she was educated and knew how to think rationally – it would be quite ungrateful to run away from the ashram. Dhaya thought that way also. But when she thought that her escape was not only an act of ungratefulness but also would be a remedy for her present predicament, she was a bit consoled. She also thought whether all ashrams would be the same; judging by her experience, she thought that all would be the same.

Renunciation meant setting aside the ways of the world and sacrificing the desires of life. That was what one learned from the discourses of the Swamiji, she thought. She also renounced all those things. She had done nothing to appease her desires so far. She had killed all her desires to satisfy those of the Swamiji. If renunciation meant that, then she too was a sanyasini, no doubt.

It was Chandini who showed her the way to escape. She searched or rather was destined to search for a new way through renunciation, tolerating everything, like her. The world outside was full of colours – the inmates of the ashram, who were the friends of darkness, must be freed to enjoy those colours – it was Chandini who sermonised so first.

Dhaya could not help asking her the question, "Sister, don't you need that freedom?" She knew that answers were waiting for the questions.

"My dear young lady, my age doesn't allow me to enjoy the life that was full of those colours! I am imprisoned in these dark rooms and have been withered out and darkened by Time. All my colours have vanished and I've become quite colourless. My colourlessness would frighten the colours outside." When Chandini said those words, she sobbed; in her looks there was the helplessness that told one that there was no change left in her life.

After that, Dhaya did not ask anything. She thought that she should not make Chandini weep. She felt that every inmate of the ashram was the symbol of a sinned soul. She thought that the only way to escape from such thoughts was to run away from the ashram.

She must run! The only target left to her was the end of that run. It was that end that was waiting for her in all her journeys through all her generations. "Why should I worry when there is no one to call me back or to love me?" she asked herself.

"Freedom 'from her father'" – that was the reason behind her coming to the ashram. She was pestering her mother to tell her where her father had gone. One day, when she could no more face her questions, her mother showed a man and said, "This is your father!"

She believed that he was her father. One day, when she was helping her mother in cooking, she was blowing the wind to make the dried palm leaves catch fire quickly. The smoke and dust that came out, irritated her eyes. Tears drew a veil in her eyes.

Her hands inadvertently touched the wrong way, the plate that contained the food, ready to be served for somebody. The plate fell down spilling the food on the floor. Her mother shouted at her angrily. Then only she realised that all her mother's guests were her fathers! She was a little flower, blossomed unwantedly in the union of somebody's sperm with her mother's egg. Some truths transformed into chemicals that instigate anger and revenge. She felt that somebody had thrust into her hands, a burning piece of fire-wood. She felt that the thorny beards of her fathers and the heavily ploughed out cheeks of her mother were the worst and the most unwanted things. She also felt that somebody was droning into her ears that one should get rid of those things which weren't useful anymore and which were unnecessary ... they should be destroyed immediately.

Her mother's cheeks and eyes were completely burned in the fire. Amidst the echoes of her mother's cries, she felt that the shadows of her fathers were penetrating through her skeleton and were following her. She plunged into darkness through the back door that was open. As there was no interruption of the moon light, she ran clinging herself to the hands of darkness. That was her life's first run. That day also she had no targets to reach.

Running without any aim was the fate of her life. Before her agonies, the stars had shut their eyes. The tired legs at last found a place to rest – the ashram – a place reverberating with holy recitals.

"Amma! My Daughter!" some woman said.

Fear seized her when she heard the word, amma again.

She entered into the saffron uniform of the ashram. She wept silently when a barber tonsured her head. She wanted to say that her hair need not be removed but she did not say anything.

"I am on the first step of a life of renunciation. Let all prohibited things go!" she thought. She wanted to look at her face in the mirror just once. She had a mischievous desire to see 'Dhaya's' tonsured head.

The sanyasini, Chandini, fed her and showed her a place to sleep. She remembered just the moment she laid herself on the mat... nothing else. She was so tired, mentally too, because of the long run of the previous day.

When she woke up the next day morning she realised that her dress was crumpled.

"Oh! God! Did I sleep with my dress in such a bad shape?" she thought. She quickly picked her shirt up from the floor. She went to the class that was going on in the ashram. The swamiji was talking about the ways of life. She was listening to him. She thought that she should keep her mind and body pure. She should keep her soul pure. Her aims and plans went on developing. She realized, only, when she was in the class, that most of the inmates of the ashram were of her age.

When she returned from the class a sanyasini asked her to wash all their clothes. The clothes were too many. When she finished washing, she felt very tired.

After that, many nights had passed. Her dress was crumpled many times and was uncrumpled sometimes. Fourteen years had gone unnoticed as she worked, studied and got an

M.B.A. As she turned to look backward, she felt that Time had passed very fast. They told her that she could work in the administrative section of the ashram.

When she stepped on the wide world of the Net, she was afraid. Soon 'friendship' became some sort of a benumbing drug and she felt stumbling at times. That pushed her from the back into 'freedom', another drug.

When the doors of the outer world were opened, she could see the many colours of life. She told Chandini, "I want to go!" At first, Chandini opposed. Then she gave her consent.

Dhaya thought that later Chandini herself might have felt convinced and thought that at least Dhaya should enjoy the colours of the world outside.

Sarju had told her that he would wait for her near the mobile shop in the town. She had only a thin acquaintance with him which she had through the Web. At times, she felt shocked by his dense love. She felt that she should have met him quite earlier; she never knew that love could be so sweet. The inmates of the ashram could not know what love was at all! They'd donned the dress of darkness, she thought. She had told Sarju everything. He could love her even after knowing everything. She felt that that all her estimates of men were wrong.

When she stood in the dark corner of the mobile shop, many people turned their heads to look at her with suspicion. Some went past her and turned back to look at her again. But nobody asked her anything. "Why these people are looking at me so? Is woman only a dish of flesh? Are all her sufferings only food for their essays and stories? Some see god as an artist in woman, who had made her a thing of sexual enjoyment. Is woman a thing of beauty only to be relished? Some people feel that woman is divine. Is she only a lifeless statue, to be worshipped at?" she pondered.

"Who is woman and who's not?" When she was waiting for Sarju, such questions popped up in her mind. Her eyes riveted on the Omni van that went past her and stopped at a distance. Her eyes noted the van's number: M.H. 18A 1289. "The van was registered in Mumbai," she thought, "Sarju came out of the back seat with a smile. That was the moment, when she knew for the first time in her life, what happiness was! She thought that she was the luckiest woman in the whole world. Of course, she was a bit afraid on seeing the dark faces inside the van. Her legs pulled her back, involuntarily. "Sarju told me that he would come alone… then why so many people?" she asked herself. There was some unknown fear lurking in her mind as though she saw the shadows of her mother's husbands were hiding in them … as though she smelt the odour of the sanyasis of the ashram in them.

But without knowing how she was pulled in and thrown into the back seat of the van forcefully, her mind was wandering as the van sped up.

Notes

1. amma: mother, also a term of motherly love and affection. Sometimes girl children and even grown-up girls are addressed as 'amma', by elders out of extreme affection.
2. sanyasi: a monk.
3. sanyasini: lady-monk.

Clay Butterflies

Kunhanandan master was tired… he was fed up with looking at the walls. The walls were all painted with the same colour. Even the roof and the floor were of the same colour. Sometimes, he even thought of switching the T.V. on to while away the time. But the T. V. programmes too were boring. Nothing was new. That town, which was bereft of any variety, was monotonous... there was nothing strange. Kunhanandan teacher who was a lover of colours, was fed up with the colourless town. There was nothing fresh or strange in the town; it was stale. He thought that nothing was so bad as loneliness.

He was brought there, just as a change from his lonely life in Thurayurkkara. In Thurayurkkara, loneliness was his friend only during nights. During the day time, he had the company of his 'disciples' and friends. Whenever he went to the market, the people there adjusted their dhoties as a mark of respect for him. On such occasions, he felt elated. At such times it appeared to him that his greatest asset was his battalion of disciples and friends. Whenever he took tea at the tea-shop, the people assembled there vied with one another to pay for his tea. Even if he wanted to walk for some distance, his disciples did not allow him. They 'bundled' him either on their bikes or in their cars. The teacher was the first comer whether it was a marriage or a death. He had come to this big town breaking that big circle. In fact, he did not want to do so. It was his son, Manu, who had compelled him to come there. Manu thought that it was not good for his father to lead a life of loneliness there.

But he never felt lonely there. After Vasantha had left him he had the work of bringing Manu up. He wanted him to become a teacher. But somehow Manu became an engineer. He never thought that Manu would leave Thurayurkkara, even though he had become an engineer. It was god's will that he had become an engineer, he felt. Vasantha too ran away with an engineer. Manu was then just four years old. When she decided that she did not need Manu too, he deeply hated her.

After Sarala teacher's death, Manu became much worried. His father and Sarala teacher retired in the same year. The teacher's children-all of them – became doctors. Sarala teacher became friends with Death at a silent moment in a night in the long journey of life. Perhaps Death might have asked her in the backyard of her house, "Do you want to see your children?" Death was always like that. Sometimes, it gave concessions! But Sarala teacher never liked concessions. She always used to throw them away. That was why she ignored the concession put before her and asked Death, "Why should I wait for those doctor-children who has no time even to phone me? Don't waste time! Convert me into my husband, Shankar's shadow immediately!"

"Death shows all its magic and light, spreads its fragrance gently and separates slowly the life from the body. It seems at times, that Death is a never drying spring of Love. Often Death is in love with man. That love unites man with Death. The people who do not understand this, say that life has come to an end," he thought.

After that, there was only a congress of worms in the teacher's body. For forty five days her body lay without anybody's knowledge and without getting its last rites done.

Perhaps the teacher's soul, that could not enter the heaven, might have flown to her children and pleaded, "Children! Please bury my body so that I may enter heaven!"

Her doctor – children who knew how to read the rhythms of the hearts of their patients, had no time to know the heart- beats of their mother or to understand the agony of her soul.

Another truth was that they could not get any money from that patient. Anandan teacher suddenly stopped the flow of his thoughts. He thought that the thoughts one had when he was alone, could change one's view of the world.

Manu, was not like Sarala teacher's children. He phoned many times daily. It was only to wipe his worries out, Kunhanandan master had agreed to come to that town.

The master locked his room. The key had to be left in the office. So, there was no need to worry. Mobile phone was a blessing! He had not decided where to go. He had gone many times to the shopping mall with his son. Whenever he went there, he used to think why so many people were loitering there! The sights were all the same – quite boring! There, wherever one turned his eyes on, one could see only things and things! Earlier, man used to go in search of things! Times had changed

– in the present day world, things came to his hands. All things, both necessary and unnecessary, were arranged in rows in the mall.

He had heard about Kamathipura earlier. "Why not go there?" he asked himself. The Red Light area! How did that area get that name, he asked himself. Many questions floated in his head.

"Is it because of the red blood that oozed out of the

virgin's vagina in the first encounter? Or is it because of the blood that comes out during ladies' periods?" the master pondered over.

Suppose, if Manu saw him on the way? Then a cloud of suspicion would hang over him forever. After Vasantha had left him, he remained chaste. Reading and writing were his only love.

In the beginning, many people tried to convince him to get married again. But he did not marry anybody. It was not because of his love for Vasantha; rather, he thought that he did not need to be humiliated yet another time.

Vasantha should be leading a comfortable life. Her children would have grown up… like Manu. Were they not his brothers and sisters?

Manu had never asked him about his mother. He also did not tell.

On his betrothal day an old man asked about his mother.

"She's dead!" His immediate reply silenced him. He did not feel like saying that she's alive. "A mother is not only a reality, that never vanishes. Beyond that, she's somebody who gives happiness to one's heart and soul! The truth is that when that happiness goes, she also becomes dead even though she's physically alive! If a mother gives love, she never dies!" he thought.

When he was walking on the pavement, a dust – filled and rusted iron board with the words 'Kamathipura' crossed the teacher's eyes without his permission.

"Let me go and see!" he decided.

He thought that that was the uglier side of the town. He saw fatherless children playing, kicking the ditch water. The foul smell coming from the ditch troubled his nose.

The condoms were floating in the water like paper-ships. The water was grey due to the mixture of semen and dirt. A customer came out, opening a small door. The teacher could see the stains of semen on his pants. There was a sense of guilt in his face. The ladies who were standing in the street invited the teacher.

There were young girls from 15 to quite beefy figures. They wore only bikinies and banians above their knees. They have dusted their face white. On their lips there was heavy lipstick.

He was disgusted. "Beauty, only when it is natural, is a thing to be relished," he told himself. Without minding their welcome gestures the master went on walking. His legs stopped when somebody spat some saliva, coloured with betel leaves, in front of him. He stopped to see who she was.

She was a plump lady with big eyes and a big thilak on her forehead. She was a bit different from others with a fair complexion. Instead of lipstick, she had given a red tinge to her lips with betel leaves. There were four folds in her neck. She was wearing a sleeveless banian and put her hands beyond her neck so that the thick hair in her armpits were visible. Her big breasts were trying to jump out of the thread – chains of her banian. As she was standing, putting her one leg on the other, the teacher could understand that she wore no clothes under her bikini.

He turned his head suddenly as though he had seen

something which he should not have seen at all – as though a needle was thrust into his iris. "Why these people volunteer themselves as commercial products? These people have heavy make-up and are sitting like the products arranged in rows in the malls. Who have made them broiler chickens?" he asked himself.

Kunhanandan master walked fast forward. That lady scolded him in filthy language.

The teacher felt uneasy. He thought that he should not have come there at all.

He exited through a small lane. It seemed that that was a street for old prostitutes. There were ladies aged more than fifty. With their dry skin that appeared as though it was covered with a coat of mud and with their bones quite transparent, they were standing there. On their heads, they wore strings of withered flowers. The master would not think that they were prostitutes.

They were standing in rows. Manu's construction company's site was somewhere nearby, he remembered. He was afraid.

A woman, more than fifty, taking 'out' her two lean and dried breasts, invited him: "Sir, only five rupees sir! I have nothing to eat sir!"

Poor creature! She would not have taken any food, the teacher thought. He took a five rupee note from his pocket and tried to give it to her. His eyes met hers. Kunhanandan master jerked backward as though the like poles of magnets repel each other away

.

There was the same black spot in her eyes as in

Vasantha's.

She took the coin with a swing, and 'extended' her breasts to him.

"If you want, hold them; otherwise leave!"

Malayalam words in a Red Light area! He looked at her again in order to ascertain that it was Vasantha! Yes! It was she! He started walking away from that place.

Kunhanandan master only thought that the sun was waiting on the other side of the evening for yet another rise!

Notes

1. dhothi: unstiched garment for men that hangs from waist to ankle.
2. 2.thilak /pottu:. a round mark put on the forehead (as a sign of auspiciousness or beautification).

The Tsunamic Dance of God

"Whoever you are, please come inside!" he told so to express his inability to get up from his bed. Earlier, when he was in his village or abroad, he was always like that. He was a writer and it was his habit to invite everybody into his house and talk to them, whether he came to see him as his fan or he was just a street vendor! But now it's different – he invited everybody because of his inability. He was living in a room in the upstairs at present.

A tall young man came in. On his fair face there was a black moustache. His beard had many curls – it appeared quite short. May be that was the fashion of the day. Time expected from the young, different fashions at different times. His uncombed hair was drawn to the front. His hair style was expressive of his playful nature and the purity of his heart.

Perhaps the foul smell that emanated from the room might have disgusted him. He did not suspect without any reason. How many days had gone since he had become bedridden – he had to pass motion and urine in the bed itself! Because of the foul smell, the young man tried to close his nose but his heart would not allow him to do so. The young readers who read his stories which he had written during his good times

– when he had time and when he was healthy, came to bathe him. At such times he remembered the days when he swam and bathed in the river. Even after he had returned from abroad, he used to go and swim in the river. Such times brought the memories of seas he had seen abroad. He used to spend his weekends not in taking brandy or whisky but in swimming in the sea. All his swimming 'adventures' – lying on his back or with his face and chest down, were unforgettable memories.

He could not see the visitor's face clearly. "Who's he?" he asked himself. His sight also was poor. One eye had completely blocked his sight; another was like a half-opened window.

He held his hands and mumbled: "kaka!" "Adhi Dev!"

He needed nothing to recognize him. Everybody used to address him affectionately 'uncle,' ikka, or mama.

Only his sister and he used to address him kaka. In those days, he used to laugh whenever they addressed him so. But today it had become a mark to recognize somebody.

When everybody in the Gulf spoke with a different accent, mixing English, that family alone used the tongue of Chamravattam.

When the young man tried to sit on the bed, he prevented him saying, "No! No! It's stained with urine!" But Adhi did not hesitate to sit even after he told him so.

When his lifeless hands were held by Adhi's hands throbbing with life, fresh air peeped in as a symbol of the joy of Nature. When fresh air came in, it seemed that music itself came in.

The same music he used to hear in Ajman beach! Then Adhi Dev was ten and Minnu was six. Their father Vaishakhan and mother Chandramathi were enjoying their second honey moon in the beach. Like the stories his friend Vaishakhan wrote, his heart was overflowing with love.

Before he married Chandrmathi, he had some affairs. After the marriage, he had to have some restrictions. That truth was a secret known only to her and his lady loves.

As he had no children, he loved Vaishakhan's children very much. Whenever they ran backwards, competing with the waves, they held his hands tightly. Once he ran into the sea dragging Adhi along with him.

Immediately Minnu began to cry: "Take me also to the sea!" For a few minutes he stood with the children in the sea water, guarding them against the waves of the sea.

Sensing the silence that pervaded the whole house and searching it with his eyes, he asked, "Where is aunty?"

Last Monday we had her 40th. day ceremony. That was all what he said. Silence reigned between them. The young man smiled at the question that fell out suddenly: "Do you know how did the sea water become salty?" That was a smile filled with worry!

When he was a boy he was full of such questions. His little heart thought that kaka was an encyclopaedia.

"Yes!" a short answer.

"How long are you like this?" Adhi asked.

"More than one and half a year," the old man replied.

"Kaka, what happened to your novel?"

He thought that the talk about stories and novels blocked the flow of blood in his nerves. The blood had already frozen in many nerves. Sometimes, he thought that if the blood flow would stop completely, he could stop passing urine and motion in the bed.

Like his mind, his stomach also had made a truce with hunger. His wife used to stand near the dining table and look at him eagerly as he relished the food she served him. Her tasty food had made him, her slave. Whenever he praised her for her taste, he experienced a rare sense of joy. Before he realised that it was a purer kind of joy to relish her food than being a writer, she had gone! At times, he also served her food. That was also a pleasant experience. However much he ate the food she cooked, he never felt satiated. As he had a lean physique, he never became plump!

She used to ridicule him, "However much you take, you never become plump!"

In return, he used to look at her face and smile. She left him even without saying goodbye. She knew earlier, when he was abroad, that his heart was not strong enough to withstand the shock of her departure. That was why she left him all of a sudden, after preparing the lunch.

She had told him that she had borrowed some rice from their neighbour. That 'loan' he could not repay yet.

"Whether she would get her punishment in kabar or not, I don't know! O God! Had I seen my neighbour I would have pleaded my inability to repay the loan!" he thought.

Adhi asked, "Wasn't the novel finished yet?" That question gave him some solace. Thoughts froze in his heart.

"After returning from abroad, we were running from one hospital to another, for a child. We sold everything we had … the doctors were becoming richer and richer!

When we realized that the children were safe in the hands of god, it was already too late. When my life emigrated into the world of writing, I realised that there was no need for a separate life-story!"

The copy of the novel might be lying amidst her saris or amidst the bundles of books. When the big house was sold there was no space for keeping the books. Her saris and maxis had become book shelves.

Sometimes termites entered through the doors of the thatched house to read the books. There were snakes too, which died of reading his books. The hens pecked those snakes among the books. The hens never read books! It was a surprise that he searched for the book packets and brought them before him.

The termites had already edited the words and sentences that needed editing.

He laughed.

The papers contained facts related to a place.

"I'll bring out this book!" said Adhi.

"What's Vaisagan doing?" he asked, as a reply.

"We could not see him often after he became the president of the academy. We know that he is alive only through his photos and writings that appear in papers and special numbers!"

He liked his joke. Bubbles of laughter burst in his heart.

"Don't you need to go? Chamaravattam is far away. Won't Chanadramathi be worried, if it's too late?"

"Um". That 'um' was the whining of a man who had become a slave of Time!

Kaka! He wanted to ask something but he froze his words in his throat by swallowing his saliva.

"It's O.K!" He said as though he had understood his mind. Shouldn't a writer have the ability to understand the feelings of others?" But even his own pen would not come forward to pen down his trials and tribulations.

"I'm happy that I could at least see you!"

Adhi said hesitantly, "Old age home?"

"A good book. I've read it! But I don't need it now!" Adhi gave out a hearty laugh. His half-opened eyes saw the waves of laughter bursting between his white teeth. "Would you please take me to the estuary?"

"Where's it?"

"The sea shore, like the one in Ajman!"

He had opened the flood gates of joy. With a heart completely filled with love and affection, he prepared him to take him for an outing.

He cleaned the stains of stools with coconut – fibres. He bathed him and found out for him a dhoti and a shirt from a bundle of clothes his wife had washed earlier and kept folded neatly.

Adhi carried him to an auto. He could see the colourful scenes of Nature that came out, pushing the curtains aside. The sperms which did not materialize as children, were hung inside the glass tubes. They, which should swim fast competing with one another, were standing motionless.

"Kaka, the estuary!" He didn't need the information at all. The duets of Love and the smell of the sea could be felt even from miles far away.

The children who had come with their mothers, were playing there. Some of them were holding eagle kites in their hands.

The eagle kites were flying all over the sky, like the life that was flying round and round the world. The little angels were pulling them down with threads whose edges could not be seen from the ground. It was like god playing kites with human lives.

The sea was calm. That was a sight not seen so far.

The sea breeze gave out the smell of traditional medicine.

His legs that had been quite lifeless so far, started pulsating with life.

He could put his legs slowly on the sand.

"Kaka!"

Belief and expectation were on Adhi Dev's face. He did not say anything.

He was steaming with enthusiasm as he walked forward.

"Adhi! My dear boy! You wrote 'sea-mother' on the sea sand and the sea waves came and wiped it out...do you remember?"

He laughed and said, "Yes!"

"I should tell Vaishakhan that the title of a life-story is written on the sand: 'The Tsunamic Dance of God!' It should be picked up before the mother of sea wipes it out!"

The waves came fast; they became thinner and thinner as they came nearer and nearer! He walked forward in staggering steps, with his legs which had been lifeless till then!

Notes

1.dhothi: unstiched garment for men that hangs from waist to ankle.

2.ikka: brother.

3.kabar: tomb/grave.

4.kakka: uncle.

5.mama: uncle.

Yours Wholeheartedly,

He saw his reflection in the mirror. There was more grey hair. The grey hair reminded him of his age. Even then, he could not pluck and throw away the love that had entered into his heart as a guest.

He was continuously waging a war in his heart.

Deva had told him that he could remember her face whenever he felt depressed. But her face was always in front of his eyes. Many a time, he thought that he should not think about her. But wherever he turned his eyes on, there were her face and her paintings.

Whenever he saw any tall, fair lady in a sari, he could only think of Deva.

The spring of love in him had dried out a long time ago and its orifice had been sealed tight and hard with clay. Now there was a hole in it!

He fell in love for the first time when he was studying pre-degree. That was with Indhu! They travelled together throughout their school and college days. Once he mustered all his courage and told her about his love. But he was a bit too late! She had already woven a bridge with love-threads to a boy who had run in the race just before him! Afterwards, he did not fall in love with any other girl. Moreover, there grew an intense hatred in him against Love. It appeared to him that Love was a decayed state of mind that had to be buried forever at the time of marriage.

He thought that he should go to a saloon and dye his hair with black henna. The next day was the day to meet Deva. He had seen her only twice in a year. Those meetings with her ran as reflections, in his mind.

As he was doing his usual work of proof reading, he suddenly saw that news! It said that there would be an exhibition of one Deva's paintings in the Tagore Centenary Hall, on the 25th.

"Who's this Deva?" he enquired his colleague, Santosh.

"She's a young painter! She was in Delhi for a long time. That's why nobody here knows her," Santosh told him assertively.

There was not much crowd in the Tagore Centenary Hall. It was a Sunday – there should have been some crowd. There wasn't any other programme in the town. Many people had come to see Rekha's recent exhibition. Of course, there was some magic in her lines. Nothing else! There wasn't anything unique in them. But the newspapers and magazines had given her exhibition a wide coverage. Perhaps, Rekha might have had some influence over reporters and writers. She was in good terms with them, he thought.

"Haven't you invited all? The crowd is quite small!" he asked Deva.

"I don't know many people here! I just informed the newspapers only." She replied.

"Your paintings demand some attention!" "Thank you! May I know your name?"

"Sivan! A proof reader in a newspaper… and you?"

"I was a graphic designer in an advertising agency in Delhi. I must seek a job here!"

"Husband?"

"In Delhi. A dentist."

"You've painted the myriad emotions that lie deeply buried in the human faces!"

Deva just smiled.

The news about that painting exhibition occupied just a small paragraph in the newspaper. But her paintings fully occupied his heart. The scenes in those paintings ran in his heart, one by one.

He got Deva's phone number from the bit of information, she had given to the newspaper. He dialled her. Their talk was filled with ramblings about paintings, literature, cinema etc. etc.

Looking at the walls of his one-roomed flat, he thought about his first night. That should have been a night of joy – a sort of realizing one's dreams. It was a happiness that sprang from the thought that the life that had been lost, had been discovered. He married Renu because of the pressure from his family and also because he did not want to waste his life. He had big expectations about Renu. He thought that she would be a good wife! It didn't take many days for him to realize that all his expectations were wrong.

When he was in a tight embrace with her and enjoying the fragrance of her body, she whispered into his ears, "I have no faith in the family system! I 'll leave you after I give birth to our first child. With the salary I get from my job in the Electricity Board, I could lead a comfortable life!"

He felt that the earth and the sky had joined together to crush him. It seemed to him that travelling through the myriad criss-crossing threads of a woman's mind would always be a distant dream!

Afterwards, he didn't say anything. He consoled himself by thinking that her words were those of an immature girl who was just married.

When she missed her periods for the first time she let out a meaningful smile. In the days that followed, Renu behaved in a self-centred way. She also looked down on him as though she had beaten him!

He even suspected that his worst enemy in one of his previous lives had become his wife in his present life. Ten months had elapsed in quarrelling and keeping silent.

When they came out of the hospital after her delivery, she asked him as though she wanted to remind him: "Do you remember what I've told you in our first night? Hereafter, there is...... nothing between us!" It needed the period of a pregnancy for her immature words to get refined. He chose his way that day without much protest at the gates of the hospital itself. It didn't take much time for the thoughts about Renu and their child to vanish from his mind.

He spent twelve years without enjoying the companionship of any lady.

While talking with Deva, sometimes she used today, "You are my talkative child!"

At such times, he felt that he was that old young man of twenty! But he never exceeded his limits when he was with Deva. His heart was filled with love that never saw a sun shine.

He dyed his grey hair black and was waiting in the Mananchira Square. Dense clouds were slowly moving In the sky.

Deva came soon without keeping him waiting for a long time. She had put a small pottu on her forehead. She was wearing a light green blouse and a sari with zari border.

The rain clouds that were beaten black and blue in the sky, danced on the earth as little drops of rain. He took shelter in her small umbrella. They walked towards the park slowly. When the rain mellowed down, they sat in a corner.

Receiving the rain drops in her hands she told, "I shall give you all my paintings!"

"Why?"

"Nothing!... I don't know how many sunrises I'd be able to see!"

"Deva! What are you saying?"

"I cannot express in words how deeply you love me! Nobody on this earth would have loved anybody as you love me!"

"So what?" he asked with eyes that were enlarged with

"I thought that I should go without telling you! Then you will search for me. When you cannot find me, you will hate me at least for a second and think: 'She has disappeared even without informing me!' I thought that you should not think about me that way. That's why I tell this! I have a wrecked heart!" She splashed her face with all the raindrops she had collected in her hands.

"What do you mean?"

"There was a small hole in the middle of my heart. They say now it has become larger. Only a little bit is left. If that too peters out…."

Sudden cough stopped her words. To have some relief from that non-stopping cough, she thrust her face into his hands for one last time.

There were snakes of blood crawling in his hands.

He saw her face, covered with an oxygen mask, through the glass doors of the I.C.U. He intercepted the doctor who came out:

"Sir?"

"Don't expect much! Heart transplant is the only way!". "Sir, My heart…"

"Um!" The doctor gave out an irritating look.

He thought that that irritating look was perhaps the expression of the doctor's inability to kill him and give his heart to somebody else.

The doctor left. It seemed to him that the shadows of the medical science stood before him and were ridiculing him. Inability, in the dress of Truth, stood before him, as though the florescent bulbs emitted black light. In the darkness, he only saw another oxygen mask, being unfastened by a nurse for a new patient.

Notes

1.henna: a reddish-brown dye that is obtained from the henna plant. It is used to colour and decorate the hands, hair, fingernails, etc.

2.pottu: a round mark put on the forehead (as a sign of auspiciousness or beautification).

3.zari: silk thread coated with silver and then gilded.

Cinderella

He got up from the bed a bit late. He had no time for breakfast.

Punctuality was very important for him. He skipped the breakfast and virtually ran to the office. Many files were waiting there for him. He had to find solutions to the problems in them. Day by day, his work-load was increasing. The previous night he had to stay in the office late. There were no fixed hours for lunch. He took food whenever there was time. It had become his habit. Life had become so mechanical…there was no place for any love or desire for duty.

If he had not so many files waiting for him in the office, if he had no computers to correct his mistakes, he would have become mad long back, existing in the prison of loneliness. That madness would have taken him to another, a purer world, of course. There, he might have a chance to see the angels in white gowns.

He ran towards the lift. A young lady with green eyes and auburn hair was waiting for the lift. He had to go down crossing seven storeys. He was now above seven skies. To reach the earth, he had to go down through those seven skies. He could see many mad people there. By the bye, what was madness? What were its symbols, he asked himself. Once, while he was walking with his father in the village, a man was smiling and talking to himself.

"Why is he talking to himself ?" he asked his father.

"He's mad!" his father replied.

From that moment, he thought that talking to oneself was a sign of madness. Another day, when he was talking to his mother chewing a candy, he saw a man walking in the street, wearing four or five pants and shirts and a turban on his head. He asked:

"Why is he wearing so many clothes, mum?"

"People who wear too many clothes around their body are mad!" she replied. Strange thoughts about madmen unknown so far sprang in his mind: "This city is full of mad people – people who wear around their bodies coats and suits and people who walk with ear phones in their ears, talking to themselves. Modern lunatics!" he thought.

The lift came and stopped in front of them as though it answered the young woman's call with green eyes and auburn hair. She stepped in and he followed her.

He examined her eyes that instigated deep love in any one. Green eyes, auburn hair, chubby cheeks, the neck with thin streams of sweat, the lips without lipstick, wearing tight jeans and kurtha and a leather bag on her shoulder – he scanned her.

"Why are you staring at me?"

"I see some uniqueness in you!"

"You need not see any uniqueness in me!" "I appreciate beauty!"

"This city is full of beautiful buildings, lawns and parks. There are many beautiful limousines. Even this lift in which we are standing is also beautiful. You can enjoy the beauty in any of them."

"There's some artificialness in all of them. Beauty, without any artificialness is God's art. I see God in such beauty!"

"O my God! Let me escape!" she said hurriedly and left as the lift showed the letter "G".

She took a taxi and mingled in the crowd. Her car was speeding towards the horizon. He extended his hand in an attempt to

catch her. But she was already out of his reach!

"I should have got her phone number!" he thought. "Had I asked her, she would have torn me into pieces with her teeth!" His body reminded him of the stark reality.

He started his car and moved in the direction opposite to her. He submitted his mind to the files and the computers in his office. There was no place for one's taste and tender heart there

– only submission.

The week end was in the grips of the intoxication of a holiday. That day, he did not touch the files, accounts and computers. He went to sleep and woke up late as he did on any other holiday. It was drizzling outside. That rain which came only once, had a rare kind of beauty. The rain in big cities was a rare bounty. Even a little rain carpeted the streets. The ground didn't absorb water at all. Did the water rebel against getting absorbed into the earth that did not align with its intentions, he thought. The municipal lorry came to suck the water in. The cold was playing games with every bone of his body. But his mind didn't experience any chill. He went to a snack bar and ordered a cup of tea. He went near a lady who was sitting on a stool in a corner. She was reading a book. He sat in front of her. She just raised her face mechanically to see who it was! As soon as he saw her face, a comforting coolness spread throughout his body.

The same girl he saw in the lift!

"You've come here too! O god! What a trouble!" she said with some irritation.

"My body shivers too much!" He told in a low tone as though he whispered into her ears.

"Don't talk unnecessary things!" she replied angrily and with some sense of pride, as though she had discovered the hidden meaning of his words.

"I've come here to sip a cup of tea to drive away the cold.

What's 'unnecessary' in it?"

She continued her reading, ignoring his words. The waiter put two sandwiches and two cups of tea in front of them. As soon as she took the first bite of the sandwich, she spat it on the table. She angrily beckoned the waiter.

"I've asked for a vegetarian sandwich. You have cheated me with a non-veg.one!"

"Oh my God! Very sorry madam. Somehow I've misplaced the sandwiches!"

"What nonsense are you talking? I am a vegetarian. You

idiot…!"

The waiter was trembling with fear when she started raising her voice …. He was afraid that his boss might notice!"

He interrupted: "It was a mistake, of course! Don't embarrass him!"

"Oh! He should not feel embarrassed, eh? I have never taken non-veg. so far in my life! But today my sanctity has been stained. It's all because of your coming here and sitting in front of me!" She kicked the floor angrily and left.

He was worried. His aim was to live without causing the least inconvenience to anybody. He wished that whenever he put his feet on the ground, he should not harm even a single ant. But today the sanctity she had maintained all her life had got stained because of his foolish act. He should not have sat there. He saw the book on the table which she forgot to take with her, when she got up from her chair and left angrily without eating the sandwich. It was 'The Last of Days' by Moris Farhi. He had searched many book shops for that book. He took the book in his hands. As soon as he turned the first page on, he saw the name, 'Cinderella' with a mobile number written under it.

That weekend holiday, he spent reading that book. Reading it in his small room under a table lamp, he completed it in a silent night. He read about Life and World. The moon and the stars joined him.

With the renewed energy the weekly holiday had given him, he drowned himself in the office – problems the next day. When there was too much work to be done, the mind would not sync with the body, would it? When he came out for lunch, his fingers moved on the numbers in his mobile.

"Hello!" a soft voice came out from his small, beautiful mobile.

"Cinderella?"

"Yes! Who's that?" The eagerness to know who it was could be felt in that voice.

"I called you just to say 'sorry' and ask for a pardon!

"Who are you?"

"It's not important who I am! What's important is what I am going to say! Moreover, I myself don't know who I am, yet!

I think that I should not harm any being in the world during my lifetime. I think that I should not harm anybody either through my actions or even thoughts. I have to make many sacrifices in order to keep myself so! I feel sorry and I tell you this from the bottom of my heart. A small negligence on my part has caused a stain on the sanctity of your habit which you've kept all these years. I know asking for a pardon or making amends would not wipe out the damage done. But I shall do anything you ask with this life that God has donated! Tell me what shall I do?"

"Is there any wound that can't be healed by Time?"

Another question came as a reply from the other end!

"I do believe that Time would heal all our wounds; still, I live with wounds that can't be cured by Time!"

"What are they?"

"Don't try to know more about me!"

"Is there no way to get out from the agony?"

"That's a remedy, not available in the market. I have one of your books… The Last of Days. Where should I bring it?" He voluntarily deviated.

"Next weekly holiday! Same time, same place!"

He disconnected the phone even without saying thanks!

"Who's he? Why's he asking for a pardon? He could have gone on in his own way. Why should I meet him next week?" she thought while attending her routine work of sending e- mails, news and photos. Among the photos she had received

that day, there was a photo of a Lebanese mother crying over the dead body of her son, killed in a missile attack by Israel.

It was she who had prepared the tour map for her brother, Robert Andrews, who had wanted to go on a world tour.

Robert used to say that the best way to know the world, to know about men and women and to enjoy pure love and unselfish affection was to travel! Her brother, who was a school teacher, kept apart half of his salary every month for going on that tour. When he bade her goodbye, she said, "Be careful while you are travelling in Kandahar. The wounds of war are still afresh there. Those people still cherish anger over the white skinned people! Moreover, hashish and opium are freely available there. Don't even touch them!"

"You need not worry about those things. What shall I bring you when I come back?"

"If you go to India, especially Kerala, you can see the ladies there using some kind of crimson and white powder to decorate their foreheads. I've seen them in T.V. serials. Buy some for me!"

Robert waved his hands to say goodbye to his mother and sister. Robert, who used to sing a hymn of love to his students, began his tour of the world with that hymn. He always liked the greenery of the Asian countries. He noticed that people who walked on the streets vanished all of a sudden. To know those countries better, he slept on their streets. One night, in the dim moon light, in the blanket of snow, he saw four shadows slowly crawling forward. He raised his head to see what they were!

Those shadows grabbed a young girl, who was sleeping with her mother on the platform of a shop. They also forcefully shut her mouth and dragged her with them. He couldn't believe his eyes.

They laid her on her back, in a lonely place where there was no one else! They tore her shirt and skirt. They removed her dress completely. When the vultures danced on her with their long and sharp nails, she gave out a piercing cry as though she would tear the whole universe into pieces.

"You please leave that girl! If you want, you can have any number of prostitutes in the streets!"

"Who're you?" The man with a long beard and wearing a kurtha and pyjama asked. Like the Afghans, he was wearing a turban whose one edge touched the bottom of his back. His eyes were reddish. He was hefty and strong.

"I am a traveller who's travelling to discover myself!" "You are a White?"

"I don't see my reflection in a mirror!"

"We are waging a holy war against the Whites. You cannot escape now!" The four joined together and surrounded Robert – they virtually built a fortress around him. Robert saw the young girl rolling up her torn shirt and skirt hurriedly and running away – that was a very soothing sight for him.

"We haven't betrayed you! It is only our Government Even now there are millions of people who support you and protest against the Government in our country. I love you and the people of your country."

"We don't have time to hear you philosophising!"

Within minutes he was crushed, by their hands. To escape from those monstrous hands, he tried to stir up in revolt every drop of blood in his body. No power in any other world or any pure force did save him.

They made him lie down on his back on the bed of the Earth. A young man among the four, took a sword from his waistband. Another pressed his two legs, another his waist and the man with a long beard pressed his head against the ground. The young man, with a sword that was drawn, looked at the man with a long beard. He received the signal from his stern eyes. The young man brought his shining sword near Robert's throat. His helpless eyes and every bit of his body searched in vain to find at least a small drop of mercy that might be hiding in those eight eyes. The young man was cutting Robert's throat with a saw. When the windpipe was broken into two, he stepped backward. Robert's soul was yearning for life like an animal that was killed for meat. For a minute, his nose and mouth opened to suck some air in.

She put the photo of the mother of that 8 year old Lebanese boy, inside her photo album. Then she had an afternoon nap, that was unavoidable in the hot world, with thoughts, burning in her heart.

After the meeting in the lift, on the second holiday day, in an evening, they were sitting at a table, opposite to each other in a cafeteria.

"I've come just to return your book!" "I've come to know you!"

"There's no need!" he blocked her.

"What's your name?"

"Sainudeen. My friends call me 'Sainu'. My erstwhile sweetheart used to call me 'Sai'!"

"Can I call you 'Sai'?"

"Only she has that right till my death!"

"I am a reporter for West Asia in The World Post!"

"You live with letters. Words are the food for the soul. As the soul eats them more and more, it becomes more and more beautiful. I am an accountant in a real estate and contract company. I live with numbers. The mischievous play of numbers was my childhood's joy! But nowadays, I see only the frightening faces of numbers!" Looking at the white sky, he let his words out slowly.

"Why do you address me in so formal a way? I'm younger than you! You can be quite informal!" She referred to the respectful way he addressed her!

That night she did not read anything in the loneliness of her room. She did not write anything either. It seemed to her that what her soul had been wandering for so far, had finally entered into her.

When he travelled with Cinderella in a four – lane high way during the last vacation he told her about his misadventure in evoking the feelings of love in the heart of a young woman.

"I gave her books. I also presented her a magazine of Poetry, the Queen of Arts. I told her that ladies don't know how to love. She replied that ladies knew only to love! I gave her some riddles. She spent days searching for the answers! She was exceptionally beautiful. She used to put a sandal pottu on her forehead. She had rosy lips. Her long hair was full of curls. Her voice was melodious. She had an exotic beauty that could not be described at all. She was like an angel! Still, I did not pay any attention to her beauty. I never enjoyed the magic of her beauty even once. Instead, I looked at her eyes that were beautifully big. I saw in them the radiant light of Love. I tried to enrich that light. I attempted to kindle her soul. But before I could reach the peak, my leave was over and I had to return. I wrote letters from this hot place. But there was no reply from her for months. Then I phoned her. She said that she had not received any letter from me. Perhaps she might have kept herself in sleeping mode or she might have feared that friendship with men beyond a certain limit is dangerous! It's OK. Now and then, I feel a little sad that she had not understood me properly. Even if she had slept with me in the same room, I would not have harmed her in any way! Never! It's because I respected her so much."

"Why do you cultivate a deep friendship with women?"

Cinderella asked with some suspicion.

"It's because the ladies are the best to pour one's sorrow out openly! If a man moves friendly with a woman, the only reward she gives him is sorrow. If a man expresses to a woman, the agony he had received at the hands of another, that agony is transformed into a pleasing pain!" he told her.

"I've never loved anybody in my life. I also don't know what the experiences of lovers are! But now when I see you, I experience a boundless joy. When I am not with you I feel lonely… I feel some kind of fear. I feel I should be with you every minute! Is this called 'love'?"

He did not answer. He drove his car without talking a word and parked it near the beach. The waves of the calm sea filled with love, were coming to the sea shore again and again. As the shore did not entertain them, they returned to the sea filled with disappointment.

"Don't love me, because you don't know anything about me!"

"I already know much! There's nothing more to know.

The waves would come to the shore again and again, no matter how many times they are rejected! The sea thinks that one day the shore may accept her. I will continue to come to you, always!"

"I am married. Even though I don't love my wife wholeheartedly, I have a wife. I want to love her at least for a minute. We each go in our own way but we still are husband and wife, legally. I loved a girl before our marriage. It was a love that went on for years! As I was unemployed then, she left me one day, to go behind a teacher. Then I went on travelling, a sort of pilgrimage undertaken with a long beard and unkempt hair, to all the temples in India. Then I got married. I decided to marry because I wanted to forget everything. But love and marriage have given me only pain! Only this loneliness gives me peace! I end up with unrequited love, every time! What can I do?"

"You may decide that love is not necessary. You can go on blaming it too as you do now! Or you can remain silent and accept it! You can even become its slave. Or, you can enjoy and be happy! As your mind thinketh, so will be your end! Once you accept love, the springs of mercy in you would open up! The flower of Love in you would bloom. Then you'll start loving everyone!"

He silently looked into her eyes. He saw some soothing tenderness in them. She was looking at the sunset for a long time.

Next day, he remained in the office like a piece of wood.

Cinderella was singing a silent melody inside him all the time.

He saw through the glass wall two uniformed police men, saying something to the young Filipino lady.

"Are you Mr. Sainudeen?" "Yes!"

"Kindly excuse us for disturbing you in the office!" a policeman told him. "Please come with us," he requested.

He shut down his computer and went with them. He did not ask them where they were taking him to. The police vehicle that sped through a four-lane highway, reached a place that was most silent in the city. It stopped in front of a building. He read the board on its gate: 'Mortuary'.

The place was filled with a quietness that was quite friendly with Death. An employee of the mortuary brought a body, put it in front of him and removed the bed sheet that covered it.

"Cinderella?"

He silently looked at that face. The green eyes were shut. The auburn hair was tied with a white cloth. The neck from where drops of sweat were oozing out, was also covered with a cloth.

"When the accident happened, the only photo that was clinging close to her chest was yours," one of the policemen told him.

"Cinderella! You were a twinkling star in my sky. When there was nothing in me that can stir you up, you went to sleep. When there's nothing new to see, why should you keep your eyes open?"

Notes

1. pottu: a round mark put on the forehead (as a sign of auspiciousness or beautification).
2. turban: a head-covering for men, worn especially by Sikhs and Muslims, made from a long piece of cloth that is wrapped around the top of the head many times.

The Trees of Sea

The night had begun to expire. The Dawn was waiting impatiently in the make-up room to appear on the stage. "Before dawn, Rakhine, the name of the place must be transformed into a distant memory. Otherwise, we cannot survive even to remember that name. The rioters would kill us!"Fathah thought.

When he started his journey, joining hands with them, he did not know anything for sure. It was Miasha who told Fathah that Rakhine would give them only Death, as a reward. Fatha loved that place with dried blood stains, only because that was the land where his ancestors lived. That was a secret, locked in his heart. When mother, father and his sister left Rakhine in a boat, they did not tell him where they were going. He also thought that he should not ask questions for which there were no answers!

"Why is this so?"Miasha asked herself. She didn't know anything about the present times and the refugees. "We are dubbed as bread beggars! We are told that we've come from Bengal!" he remembered.

"Should we transform ourselves into monkeys, then?"Miasha asked. She had some schooling. She knew something about the theory of evolution!

On hearing that question, Fathah laughed for the first time after many days. The laughter came involuntarily.

"History mocks at the Present. We have to stand as its witnesses and should fall prey to it! The Present does a post-mortem on the Past and searches for the poisonous teeth-those who had come to fill their stomach-it had swallowed unknowingly. We can say that way also!" he thought.

There was not enough darkness. It was because of the moon light. They were embarrassed that their identities were getting exposed.

There were some stars in the sky. He was angry at them who had come uninvited and were shedding some light. With the moon light, there came cries of woe and screams of pain, from somewhere.

They did not feel any sense of fear. They were used to everything. Still, his sister's blood-throbbing waist appeared in his mind as a 3-dimensional image and vanished again and again. He raised his hands over his head and held them tightly together. Existing without any strength was life's worst inability, he thought.

Miasha's looks, filled with fear, worried Fathah too! He did not say anything.

Fathah thought that they were the last bits of the firecrackers that were ignited by somebody somewhere.

A boat with an oar was waiting for them in the sea shore. They were quite old. They did not have money to purchase even them. The money they had, was stolen by Miasha, from the Baba's pocket in the ashram where she had been working.

She could not avoid thinking that Ma in the ashram might have sensed something.

When they were cleaning the kitchen Ma told her, "You have Buddha's zeal! Where ever you are, you should never forget Buddha!" On hearing those words Miasha looked at Ma with shivering looks.

"All have come to fill their stomach! The Bloody

Migrants!" she heard Baba saying loudly, in another room.

"Gowthama won't like these things!" Ma was telling again, looking at the meditating Buddha! Hiding her sleep between her eyelids, she continued, "Siddartha too has gone on wandering!"

Miasha thought that Ma knew everything and was talking covertly. When she reached the sea shore Miasha remembered Ma 's words only.

Fathah looked through a distant thin line of the shore. How deep one had to dig to get at least the skeletons of the Rohingyas which had been buried deep into the Arakan sands!

Even if they were digged out, the archaeological department might declare that those skeletons belong to the bodies of some others, not of the Rohingyas, Fathah wondered.

Fathah held Miasha's hands softly and helped her to get into the boat. When he too got into the boat, it tilted sideways. Miasha sat close to Fathah.

He saw the drops of sweat appearing near Miasha's ears even in that chill climate! It appeared to him that those drops were glittering like diamonds, in the darkness. He put his lips on her cheeks that were wet with the drops of sweat. Then he tried to steer the boat in the direction opposite to their cherished land. The waves dashed against the shore like hooting devils. Whenever a big wave came, Miasha held herself tightly against Fathah. That was a grip borne out of extreme fear that she should not go away from him. Why not she tie her legs with theirs with her dupatta, she thought for a minute. Next minute, she decided against it. It was a pilgrimage towards the Truth of Death. She knew that the remaining part of their lives had to be spent amidst the beastly waves. She also knew that any wave in love with them, would break the thin walls that existed between their Life and Death. If at least Fatha could escape, let him go, she thought. Fathah's face was full of worries. The worry that he might be leading Miasha to the gates of Death, was tearing Fathah's heart.

"Why do these people behave so? When I was a child, I used to think that all the people who are here, are Burmese. Now they say that some of us are Rohingya Muslims. They drive us away saying that we are not Burmese and our blood is different. Many a time I thought that Miasha's blood and mine are Burmese blood. But now all gather together, surround us, tear us into pieces and devour us. Aung San Suu Kyi also does not say anything about this. The happiness that followed her release has turned into an abject ridicule soon!" he thought.

When he cast a distant vision on the sea, he saw the boats which appeared as small dots. It was a travel, that was undertaken by some exiled lives in search of new shores. It was undertaken every time, searching for new islands, when people were driven away from their Islands.

"Why haven't you turned back to look at Rakhine?"

Miasha asked, breaking the silence between her and Fathah.

"Whatever I like in Rakhine, is in my heart. Why should I then turn and look back? We should not ponder over the pains of the past but anticipate the gains of the future," he replied.

In front of them were the waves of the Bay of Bengal, full of foam. But Fathah and Miasha did not even know that name, given by somebody. The sea was full of rough waves and whirlpools. They followed small boats that were travelling before them. He thought that when one didn't know the way well, it was foolish to follow those who were sailing before them. But there was no other way. In the Bay of Bengal there were more whirlpools than waves. Travelling through the whirlpools had become a struggle – the struggle to catch back life that was fast expiring!

They did not know how long they had travelled like that. They did not even notice when day changed into night and night into day.

Miasah was shivering badly even in the woollen sweater. She herself laid her withered body on his lap. Fathah removed the sweater he was wearing and covered Miasha's face and her head. He was afraid that she might catch sea – fever. He had already known about the sea-fever from his grandfather.

He recalled his grandfather's words that people would be suffering from sea – fever while sailing to Mecca and back, on the Hajj. When the fever came, it would return to the sea only after taking the sufferer's life. He also told him how they covered the dead bodies with white cloth, conducted prayers and then threw them into the deep sea with heavy pieces of iron! His uncle was lucky. He could have his burial in the soil of Rakhine. Fathah knew that the soil of Rakhine was filled with the flesh and blood of his ancestors. Only one thing he did not know: "Why are they driving us away from Rakhine?"

Miasha was in deep sleep. Nobody expected that they had to sail that long. The food and water they had brought with them were exhausted in the previous night itself. It was a long time since they had sent something to their stomachs. "Miasah is in deep sleep. How cruel I have been! I should have taken food enough to last for two or three days. I did not know then for how many days we would have to sail. What if something happens to Miasha in the mean time? The oars should be thrown into the sea immediately. Then we can lie on our backs in the boat and embrace death and have jalsamathi. I have brought her only to give her a new life. Not to throw her into the hands of Death," Fathah ruminated. He rowed the boat faster, with more energy and force. When some boats came near, he asked:

"Can I have some water please?" They bought the boats still nearer. "What happened?"

"She is not well. Fever!"

The old man with grey hair and a turban gave some water and said, "Recite fathiha and surath and then give her the water!" They went back after giving them some pieces of bread.

"Nobody knows from where help will come and who will help! When we help somebody, somebody else will help us too," he thought.

Fathah did as the old man said. He also pushed a piece of bread into Miasha's mouth. He gently touched her eyes, forehead and face.

Fathah heaved a sigh of relief only when Miasha opened her eyes. On hearing the screams from the small boats, Fathah raised his head and looked at them. Far away, there were some small glittering lights like the light emitted by glowworms.

"Some shore! I know not what shore! Miasha should be admitted into a hospital as soon as the shore is reached," he said to himself. Then only he realized that he had no money with him.

"What country is this?" That was the question that sprang up in his mind first. All boats were stopped.

A fence put up by the Navy suddenly appeared in front of them. First, he thought that it might be the U.N's peace keeping force.

"Is the U.N. duty-bound to save us?" he asked himself.

He immediately realized that it was not so. The coast guards jumped into every boat and showed the 'identity' placards of Bangladesh. They were told that the town was Teknaf. Fathah was very happy. "They kill us saying that we are Bangladeshis. These people are the heirs of our ancestors. These people would welcome and accept us!" he believed firmly. Fathah sat in the boat with some sense of birthright. "We, who had gone away from this place, have returned again to this place," he told herself.

But the coast guards, brandishing their guns asked them to go back!

Fathah shouted angrily, "Where can we go? To Pakistan, Malaysia, Thailand, India or Sri Lanka or to our Myanmar?"

Fathah realized that all boats were filled with people who were driven away from their country. Their faces betrayed their inability to enter any country.

Then he threw away the oars into the sea and laid himself near Miasha, inside the blanket that covered her. He embraced Miasha's cheeks with his face, hugged her tightly, ran his hands over her body and closed his eyes in total renunciation.

Notes

1. dupatta: along piece of cloth worn around the head, neck and shoulders by women from South Asia.
2. Baba: head of an ashram.
3. Fathiha and Surath: the first lesson of Qur'an
4. Jalasamadhi: watery grave
5. Ma: lady head of an ashram.
6. turban: a head covering for men, worn especially by Sikhs and Muslims, made from a long piece of cloth that is wrapped around the top of the head many times.

A Portrait and Some Memories

Story by: *Velliyodan*

R.K's entry into Iraq was like trespassing into a stranger's property; a transgression from Kuwait by road breaking through immigration checking and visa stamping formalities.

War has never been a novelty to people of this country, years and years of incessant battle with just a change in opponents each time. R.K's duty was to report swift and reliable news from the warfront. Athira was terribly worried when she came to know that he was planning to set off to Iraq. She argued and revolted to the level best, but all in vain.

R.K tried to console her: "If I stand reluctant to represent my newspaper, someone else will undertake the obligation and that will question my reliability. All the more, that person will also be somebody's husband or father whoever it is".

Agonies and sufferings will never have a permanent halt anywhere; it flows along like waves and ripples in a river. R.K didn't turn back and without passing a look to her, he directly went to the chief editor's cabin.

"We ought to expect utmost transparency in news from warfront only if you take the lead, R.K", precisely R.K was honoured by these words.

R.K was dumped into the Kuwait border from the where he stealthily crossed the border evading the eyes of Iraqi and American soldiers. He escaped into Mesopotamia; the much acclaimed iconic historic part of land about which he had learned long back from his history lessons.

Now it has become a place where even an ordinary farmer goes armed on his way to field. The greediness to expand the territory of one's country by conquering neighbouring boundaries had instilled unrest in the area. However, life will be peacefully flowing like a gentle stream for those with limited aspirations and wishes while other's lives will be like angry waves. This country was blessed with natural resources; competent enough with other developed countries of the world. Still, people here happened to be victims of lifelong sufferings and pain. R.K's knowledge about this nation dates back to his childhood days whilst he used to read about the war between Iran and Iraq from children's magazines. His mind flew back to olden days with every foot step; painful memories stained with blood. He felt ardent admiration for Mahatma Gandhi; that sort of admiration which he didn't feel even while leafing over his book "My experiments with truth", he who lead the country towards freedom adopting peaceful bloodless revolts. 'Mahatmaji you are a great man'; wish such a brave heart took rebirth in this desert; a much grieved society is waiting for your helping hand. R.K's accommodation was arranged in a place where journalists from different parts of the world reside. He typed his first news from warfront with shivering hands "Bomb blasts in Basra, killed many".

Loved ones of the deceased still lives bearing the pain; the raw truth felt dreadful for R.K. after mailing the captured news and pictures he sat dumb covering his face with frozen hands. Then he slowly slipped into a peaceful sleep lest in a highly unpeaceful environment.

The yankee soldiers were progressing forward dauntlessly; the inner eyes of the desert spilled tear drops moreover like blood drops polluting the eternal Tigris and Euphrates. The security guards of government treasuries were scared by the conflicts and they fled to some hiding place which made the defenceless treasuries vulnerable to attack by looters. Some carried pearls while some others stole arms and bullets.

R.K went on sending pictures from his mailbox with silent deep breaths; in between he noticed a picture which struck a deep hole in his heart, a picture shared by his Srilankan journalist friend.

R.K's momories sped past to those silent nights; those school days whilst studies were regarded as a penance, reading out lessons under the feeble glow of a smoky kerosene lamp. The picture of his mother was kept intact in his desktop about which he had cherished a myriad of pensive thoughts and memories. She had spend several sleepless nights preparing black coffee for him while he sits back late for studies; backing him with seamless moral support. R.K's mind was filled with the face he saw on the computer screen and while passing through each street devastated by bombing he was searching for none other than that particular face. Amma still lives in his memories although she had left him desolate on one cold December morning. Years later she has appeared before him in this desert clad in a Parda and that too by way of a picture. That picture was captured from Karbala and in fact that was the only information he has got about it. Karbala is miles away from Basra and journeys viaroad are not at all safe in the present scenario. If at all he dares to take the adventurous trip, it is almost sure that he would end up facing American air force cluster bombs or army's gunshots or the bomb attacks by local farmers who fight for their country's freedom besides conserving the historical remnants of it, which most often result in terrorism rather than a freedom fight. Still, a return back without meeting that mother would be like neglecting the favour that God has granted him to meet his own deceased mother. May be he will never get an opportunity like this anymore in life. Even though there is no guarantee that he could achieve his wish, he decided to take a try.

R.K tucked his belongings including all his tools; a laptop, camera and also a packet of bread, ketchup and a bottle of water into his carry bag. He set to Karbala yet not sure whether he could complete his journey or not. He climbed on a truck carrying vegetables, curled into a little loop among the vegetable baskets and folded himself uncomfortably. He examined the vegetables; all have lost its freshness. When the blasting become severe and hazardous the journey gets interrupted in between which may prolong for days and weeks and that might have made these vegetables rot like this. He saw a migrating family too in the truck boarded from Najaf going elsewhere; an old man with his wife and children fleeing to some distant land where they can find peace. R.K felt like telling him, "what you are searching is inaccessible"; but he gulped his words which appeared like a hard lump in his throat. R.K comforted himself by assuming that vehicles carrying food stuff will be free of any threat; nevertheless it didn't happen. It was a small town on the banks of Euphrates.

Local citizens were not seen anywhere, the houses on either sides of the road were dark and silent. All of a sudden, the truck stood frozen in front of few armed soldiers. They climbed up and started searching for hidden arms among the vegetables throwing them carelessly here and there. Even though they failed to recover anything they took the truck, driver and the family under their custody. But R.K was left to go as he is an Indian. The perpetual silence manifested by government of India in matters which are of no importance to them sometimes helps its nationals to slip away from snaring situations like this; yet it provoked a sense of self-reproach devouring the humanism in him.

R.K couldn't hold his instincts to talk to the soldiers on behalf of that family; but how? The soldiers behaved as though they were aliens.

In fact no soldier will keep a record of how many people he had killed during his service other than firing gunshots on whoever happened to come against his way; some may be killed few may get saved.

R.K colligated that with an incident in his home on a summer afternoon when he found a cobra in sound sleep inside his bathroom; it has taken abode there in its search for a cool place to rest. Apart from disturbing it, R.K allowed it to wade back to its burrow even after his wife's repeated pleads to kill it as he felt that these creatures are also playing an important part in maintaining the balance of nature. Here human beings are deprived from their right to live in their own birth place! Where will the soldiers take that family to? May be to some infamous jail where they may be stripped on the pretext of security checking and interrogation. R.K walked straight through some distance and there came a car carrying a pilgrimage group from Koofa heading towards Karbala. A similar pilgrimage took place years back under the leadership of Imaam Hussain whose travel from Koofa was of great historical significance. When the pilgrimage group reached Karbala, he was decapitated by Yaseed's army. The victorious procession with Imaam's decapitated head has created revolutionary impact in the people of the city. R.K gobbled his dried bread and ketchup whilst in the vehicle, his body being tired like his mind. The soil smeared red by Imaam Hussain's blood yearned for blood to quench its thirst; that may be the reason why this land is never free of war. Women and children were kept in a refugee camp in Karbala. Their eyes shone with hope on hearing that R. K was a reporter from India.

"Will you please tell the rulers of your country to save us?"

What could R.K reply as he clearly knows that he would never be able to present their request in his country where he is not even a local panchayat member?

He simply buried it all in his heart and left without further speech.

He could see small children desperately trying to suckle milk from barren breasts and on finding them empty they bite them hard; the mothers left to suffer the pain uncomplainingly. R.K's eyes went through each and every woman in the camp lest he failed to find the ace he searched for. Someone told, today morning also there was heavy bomb showers in that area killing many women. May be she also....? An intuition of meeting his mother has taken him here; will it come true?

R.K stepped out from the refugee camp with unaccomplished hopes and wishes. "valadhee...valadhee..." Wailing voice of a mother attracted R.K's attention to that direction. From a gown resembling darkness only her face and forearms could be seen outside. She was looking at the stars in the sky and crying, "My son my beloved son". The entire situation appeared to him as though every being in nature has lost its capacity to react; not even a single star responded her wails! R.K moved forward to hold and comfort her. "They ...they took my son.." He could perceive that she was trying to trace her son's remains among dead bodies charred by bomb blasts. And from his cupped hands, her face adhered to the camera lens from where it flew away to some distant land.

The Baby Sitter

In her solitary confinements, his innocent smile sprinkled droplets of happiness. The undefined dark spread epochs of her life were turned into colourful expressions by the presence of the little one.

Being a woman denied with the fortune to shower motherly affection, she always cursed her fate...or curse herself for what she is. Sometimes God is like that. He sets apart certain pleasures for some while some are selectively deprived of certain things. Facing her mirror she used to ask her belly which castles an amputed barren womb "Will there be a life budding inside me? Is there any cocooned pupa getting ready to spread its tiny wings and fly out?"

All these questions floated around her as unanswered puzzles. The time machine never waits for anyone. It travels along the fixed path without showing any consideration to the world that runs on its needles.

She remembered the prayers of her wellwisher's while leaving India. All of them wished her with nice words ..."when you come back you will never be alone, all our prayers are with you"....Everyone blessed her for her dreams to come true. The climate and atmosphere in middle east may create a favourable change in her. The rays of hope kindled in her lit bright for sometime. But all these remained as bare hopes.

Once she asked her better part "Why God is not opening His eyes to my calls.?"

"No, dear, we are so special for Him. "he comforted her. "Then why is it like this?" She frowned.

Trying to force a smile over his face he said " The much anticipated happiness that comes late in life will be more rewarding."

She tried to imagine what is going through the mind of the man beside her. How hopefully he tries to make her spirits lighten. She used to say often " If I give birth to a child, I will make him a physician who has the ability to communicate with ailing hearts."

But all her aspirations remained dry without the faintest speck of hope. To put a halt to her moments of loneliness, she decided to work as an aaya for a small child. At first her husband refuted but later yielded to her interest. Yet he warned her with a couple of words "At the end you will be left out just as an aaya, the kid will leave you one day or other."

"At least there is one consolation. Even though it is a matter of few hours, he will consider me as his own mother and cuddle close to me. That would be enough to contend me." She soothed her distress with a long breath.

There upon her days were filled with a state of euphoria. She gets up early morning, cooks food, cleans the house, washes the clothes and anxiously waits for the clock to struck nine. Once the doorbell rings a thousand wings buds out from her body and she flies to the door to grab the child from his mother. Not only her, he is also eager to incline to the warmth of her chest and free himself from his mother's snowy hold. In the days ahead, her husband was happy to hear her humming sweet flavours of lullabies from the kitchen and bathroom.

The innocent fragrance emanating from his cute smile took her to a curious world where she has never been into. A world devoid of hatred, jealousy and competition. A world where all are alike, free of pain...where the heart feels like a feather. She was entirely transformed to an infant, a return back to childhood fantasies.

After a day of scheduled office chores, when his mother returns to snatch the child from her a feeling of spite dugs into the inner chambers of her heart. Many a times she wished that his mother's office time had never ended.

She took the child to the washroom teasing him, "what you need is written on your face, your aaya could read it straight baby." His eyes are like pools of naivety, free of any blemishes of hatred . Rosy lips has sensed only the taste of bottle milk. Sometimes she feels why this kid is left alone bereft of his mother's warmth? Some people may not have time to love anyone. All are in the race of life...Love, affection, fondness are getting cremated in the hunt of worldly pleasures. We are living in a world that has privileged fame, money and power. Emotional bondings are positioned in much lower rank when compared to the quest for wealth and power.

Day long sufferings, loneliness, irritating wet damp diapers, red sores are all gifted to them by their own mothers.

Necessities of human beings may differ at different ages. At this stage of infancy his need for his mother's warmth will be the single thing he desires. While approaching the twilight of life, parents may also feel the need for a shade. The loving shades of their children. At that time these children will also be in the race of life. They have grown up unaware of the value of blood relations and emotional attachments. They end up dumping their aged parents in old age homes.

While walking along the corniche on one fine holiday evening, their gaze collided with a young married couple. They were so much immersed in each other that they almost forgot the world around them even the baby in the pram which was mechanically driven by the love-struck rejoicing couple. Each time the pram's wheels bumps into some cracks on the path, the baby looks out with anxiety. Those raised eyebrows depict the insecurity cramping the child's mind. The butterfly shaped artificial nipples almost entirely covered his tiny lips. Watching the pram getting stuck in a manhole lid, she exclaimed pointing the kid " poor child, he is just a newborn infant."

"The silent communication that happens between a mother and child when the physical proximity of each other's hearts are so close can't be met by the artificial warmth of a blanket" He said.

Hearing his words she thought within herself, I will never be a mom like this, every fraction of a second will be dedicated to my child alone.

In her happy moments as an ayah , she sometimes ask the baby "why didn't you took birth in my womb?"

Then he will open his toothless mouth wide apart as if to engulf the whole of her and then both will start laughing loud. The waves radiating from their lovely smiles echoed in each and every corner of the house. She wished to carry him on her imaginary wings and fly with him to some unknown world. Despite all her sincere efforts to make him happy, his face always portrayed a mournful expression. Deprivation from the warmth of his mother's love was clearly shown on his lovely face. Being kept aloof from his birth rights haunted his feelings and he was thrown into a state of fear and awe. Sometimes he keeps on staring along the way his mother went. Then his ayah would distract his attention and picks him up and blankets him with her kisses. The presumption of losing the child's love one day or another made her husband warn her every now and then not to love the kid too much. He discouraged her by saying " never love other's kids as your own."

Inviting his attention to a lion fondling its cubs in the animal planet channel she said " even the young ones of the most ferocious animals are so gentle and lovesome. Those tender fragile faces are worth wiping away the selfish attitude of ownership and possession."

She always stood against the ones who show selfishness towards the love for children. Her love for children was beyond the barriers of colour, language and province.

Several days passed after the vacation...,, the child and his mom was not seen she worried a lot.. is he sick or what???!!!!

She called up his mom but the response was not so impressive and she disconnected the phone abruptly. She felt the darkness seeping into her eyes, the silence filling in the room plagued her emotions.

While coming back from office, her husband's face was also found gloomy and desolate. Is it because of the absence of the child??

She verbalised her emotions "his mother is not going for work now?"

He nodded in affirmation.

"then."

In response he held her close to him. How could he tell her that his mom doesn't want her child to be looked after by an ayah who speaks in her local language or mother tongue. In fact, his mom wants her child to be with an English-speaking modish babysitter whom she already found out for him. Hiding this truth from her he replied "let us return back home dear."

www.ingramcontent.com/pod-product-compliance
Lightning Source LLC
Chambersburg PA
CBHW021340060726
47591CB00006B/2110

* 9 7 8 1 7 3 8 4 3 2 2 2 6 *